Tolley's Income Tax 2017
Post-Budget Supplement

D0279452

Tolley's Income Tax 2017 Post-Budget Supplement

by

David Smailes FCA

Tolley®

Members of the LexisNexis Group worldwide

United Kingdom	RELX (UK) Limited trading as LexisNexis, 1–3 Strand, London WC2N 5JR
Australia	Reed International Books Australia Pty Ltd trading as LexisNexis, Chatswood, New South Wales
Austria	LexisNexis Verlag ARD Orac GmbH & Co KG, Vienna
Benelux	LexisNexis Benelux, Amsterdam
Canada	LexisNexis Canada, Markham, Ontario
China	LexisNexis China, Beijing and Shanghai
France	LexisNexis SA, Paris
Germany	LexisNexis Deutschland GmbH, Munster
Hong Kong	LexisNexis Hong Kong, Hong Kong
India	LexisNexis India, New Delhi
Italy	Giuffrè Editore, Milan
Japan	LexisNexis Japan, Tokyo
Malaysia	Malayan Law Journal Sdn Bhd, Kuala Lumpur
New Zealand	LexisNexis NZ Ltd, Wellington
Singapore	LexisNexis Singapore, Singapore
South Africa	LexisNexis Butterworths, Durban
USA	LexisNexis, Dayton, Ohio

ISBN for this volume: 9780754553779

Printed and bound in Great Britain by Hobbs the Printers Ltd, Totton, Hampshire

Visit LexisNexis at www.lexisnexis.co.uk

About This Supplement

This Supplement to Tolley's Income Tax 2016/17 gives details of changes in the law and practice of UK income tax from 2 September 2016 to 7 March 2017. It lists the changes in the same order and under the same paragraph headings as the annual publication. Also included is a summary of the proposals made in the Chancellor's Budget on 8 March 2017.

Each time Tolley's Income Tax 2016/17 is used, reference should be made to the material contained in this Supplement. The Contents give a list of all the chapters and paragraphs which have been updated.

Contents

Spring Budget 2017

1

Allowances and Tax Rates

See Spring Budget 2017 for allowances and tax rates for 2017/18.

Scottish rate of income tax

[1.9] The second and third paragraphs are replaced with the following:

'In fact, on 11 February 2016 the Scottish Parliament agreed to set the Scottish rate at 10% for **2016/17**, with the result that Scottish taxpayers will pay income tax for that year at the same rates as other UK taxpayers. Income tax throughout the whole of the UK will continue to be collected and administered by HMRC. HMRC has published a technical note 'Clarifying the Scope of Scottish Income Tax Powers' (www.gov.uk/government/uploads/system/uploa ds/attachment_data/file/573519/FSITP_TechNote.pdf).'

Under the sub-heading 'Future development', the text is updated to read as follows:

'*Scotland Act 2016, s 13* goes further than the above in that, with effect for **2017/18** onwards), it amends *Scotland Act 1998, Pt 4A* so as to empower the Scottish Parliament to set its own income tax rates and thresholds for Scottish taxpayers (as defined above) independently of, and not linked to, UK rates. Based on the Scottish Government's Budget presented on 15 December 2016, the rates and thresholds for Scottish taxpayers will be the same as those for other UK taxpayers *except* that the higher rate threshold will be £31,930 (as opposed to a figure of £33,500 for the rest of the UK). There are no restrictions on the rates or thresholds that the Scottish Parliament can set, except that it cannot set different rates for different types of income. All other aspects of income tax will remain in the power of the UK Parliament, including the imposition of the annual charge to income tax, the personal allowance, the taxation of (and rates of tax on) dividend and savings income, the ability to introduce and amend tax reliefs and the definition of income. Liability to the dividend ordinary, upper and additional rates will be determined by reference to UK rate thresholds. CGT rates (see **11.3** CAPITAL GAINS TAX) will be determined as if a Scottish taxpayer paid income tax at UK rates. Income tax throughout the whole of the UK will still continue to be collected and administered by HMRC. [*Scotland Act 1998, Pt 4A; Scotland Act 2016, s 13; SI 2016 No 1161*].'

Income tax in Wales

[1.10] The second paragraph is updated to read as follows:

'Originally a referendum was required to be held throughout Wales on whether or not the Welsh Assembly should make use of the above power. This requirement has now been abolished. [*Wales Act 2014, ss 12, 13; Wales Act 2017, s 17*].'

Indexation of personal reliefs and tax thresholds

[1.17] The text is updated to read as follows:

'The basic rate limit, the starting rate limit for savings, the personal allowance, the married couple's allowance, the blind person's allowance and the income limit for age-related allowances are increased by the same percentage as the percentage increase (if any) in the consumer prices index (CPI) (for 2015/16 onwards, previously the retail prices index) for the September preceding the tax year over that for the previous September. The resultant figures in the case of the basic rate limit and the income limit for age-related allowances are rounded up to the nearest £100 and in the case of the starting rate limit and the personal reliefs to the nearest £10.

The new figures are specified in a statutory instrument by HM Treasury before the tax year begins, but no change is required in PAY AS YOU EARN (52) deductions or repayments before (normally) 18 May in the tax year.

The above automatic increases may be varied by Parliament by means of the annual *Finance Act*. See **1.18** below for the freezing of age-related personal allowances for 2013/14 onwards.

It was intended that, in future, the amount of the personal allowance should equal the yearly equivalent of the adult national minimum wage (NMW) at the start of the tax year in question. This was to take effect in the tax year immediately after that in which the allowance first reached the level of £12,500. It has since been announced that this planned linkage of the personal allowance to the NMW is to be scrapped (Autumn tax update, 5 December 2016 at www.gov.uk/government/publications/finance-bill-2017-draft-legislati on-overview-documents/overview-of-legislation-in-draft at para 1.4).

[ITA 2007, ss 21, 57, 57A; FA 2012, s 4(6)(8); FA 2014, ss 2(8)(9), 4; FA 2015, ss 3(3)(5), 5(10)(11); F(No 2)A 2015, ss 3, 4].'

Examples on allowances and tax rates

[1.23] Example (iv) has been revamped, and a new Example (v)(c) has been added. Example (iv) is technically correct, and in accordance with the equivalent example (Example 6) in the HMRC factsheet at www.gov.uk/gov ernment/publications/dividend-allowance-factsheet/dividend-allowance-factsh eet. However, a better result can be achieved for the taxpayer by setting part of the personal allowance against dividends rather than against earned income. As Example (iv) is essentially about the personal savings allowance, it has been amended by reducing the dividend income to less than the £5,000 dividend allowance. This eliminates the problem of how best to use the personal allowance in that example, but the point is now illustrated by new Example (v)(c). *ITA 2007, s 25(2)* effectively states that the personal allowance can be deducted 'in the way which will result in the greatest reduction in the taxpayer's liability to income tax'.

Example (iv) now reads as follows:

(iv) Personal savings allowance (PSA)

A single person has pension income of £36,000, bank deposit interest of £2,500 and dividends of £4,800 for 2016/17.

				£
	Pension income			36,000
(1.7)	Savings income			2,500
(1.5)	Dividend income			4,800
(1.11)	Total and net income			43,300
(1.18)	*Deduct* Personal allowance			11,000
	Taxable income			£32,300
	Taxable as follows:			
	£			
	25,000	@ 20%	(non-dividend/non-savings income net of personal allowance)	5,000.00
(1.8)	500	@ 0%	(savings income covered by PSA)	—
(1.8)	2,000	@ 20%	(savings income taxable at basic rate)	400.00
(1.5)	4,500	@ 0%	(dividends covered by dividend allowance)	—
(1.3)	32,000		Basic rate limit	
(1.5)	300	@ 0%	(further dividends covered by dividend allowance)	—
	£32,300			
	Tax payable			£5,400.00

Notes

(a) The taxpayer in this example has income within the higher rate band, but is not an additional rate taxpayer, and is thus entitled to a PSA of £500. No part of his income is actually taxable at the higher rate (due to the availability of the dividend allowance) but this is not a factor in determining the amount of the PSA.

(b) As the taxpayer has taxable non-savings income in excess of the £5,000 starting rate limit, the starting rate for savings (see **1.7** above) does not apply to any of his income. This example reflects the fact that dividend income is generally treated as the highest part of an individual's income, and savings income treated as the next highest.

(c) See (v) below for further examples on the taxation of dividends and savings income.

New Example (v)(c) reads as follows:

(c) A single person has pension income of £36,000, bank deposit interest of £2,500 and dividends of £8,000 for 2016/17.

					£
	Pension income				36,000
(1.7)	Savings income				2,500
(1.5)	Dividend income				8,000
(1.11)	Total and net income				46,500
(1.18)	*Deduct* Personal allowance				11,000
	Taxable income				£35,500

Taxable as follows:

	£			
	28,000	@ 20%	(non-dividend/non-savings income net of personal allowance)	5,600.00
(1.8)	500	@ 0%	(savings income covered by PSA)	—
(1.8)	2,000	@ 20%	(savings income taxable at basic rate)	400.00
(1.5)	1,500	@ 0%	(dividends covered by dividend allowance)	—
(1.3)	32,000		Basic rate limit	
(1.5)	3,500	@ 0%	(further dividends covered by dividend allowance)	—
	£35,500			
	Tax payable			£6,000.00

Notes

(a) In this example £3,000 of the personal allowance has been set firstly against dividend income leaving £8,000 to be set against pension income. The advantage of doing this is that it removes £3,000 of dividend income that would otherwise be taxed at the dividend upper rate of 32.5%. The cost is an additional £3,000 of non-dividend income chargeable at the basic rate of 20%. The tax saving is £375.000 (£3,000 @ (32.5% – 20%)).

(b) See note (a) to (iv) above as to the amount of the personal savings allowance (PSA).

4

Anti-Avoidance

Advance pricing agreements (APAs)

[4.27] The final paragraph is updated to read as follows:

'For detailed guidance about how HMRC interpret the APA legislation and apply it in practice, see HMRC SP 2/10 (updated 8 November 2016). The contact address for APA applications and expressions of interest is APA Lead (Nick Stevart), CTIS Business International, 11th Floor East, Euston Tower, 286 Euston Road, London, NW1 3UH (telephone: 03000 585659, email: nicholas.stevart@hmrc.gsi.gov.uk).'

Benefits from pre-owned assets

[4.45] Under the sub-heading 'Chargeable amount' and also under the sub-heading 'Intangible property comprised in a settlement', it is noted where appropriate that the official rate of interest is reduced from 3% to 2.5% for 2017/18.

Serial avoiders regime

[4.55] At the end of the first paragraph a link is provided to official guidance at www.gov.uk/guidance/serial-tax-avoidance.

5

Appeals

Alternative dispute resolution

[5.2] At the end a new paragraph is added as follows:

'It is a general rule of law that material arising from an ADR process is "without prejudice" material and cannot be used in relation to subsequent proceedings before a tribunal. See the discussion in *Ritchie v HMRC* FTT (TC 5258), [2016] UKFTT 509 (TC).'

The hearing

[5.18] At the end a citation is added to: *D v HMRC* FTT (TC 5575), [2017] UKFTT 850 (TC).

6

Assessments

Further Assessments on 'Discovery'

[6.6] Case citations are updated to read as follows: *Anderson v HMRC* FTT (TC 5092), [2016] UKFTT 335 (TC), [2017] SFTD 100; *Pattullo v HMRC* UT, [2016] STC 2043; *Miesegaes v HMRC* FTT (TC 5129), [2016] UKFTT 375 (TC), [2016] SFTD 719.

Immediately above the paragraph beginning 'Where an agreement has been made under *TMA 1970, s 54* to settle an appeal', a new paragraph is added as follows:

'The condition in (2)(a) above is met only if there is a causal link between the loss of tax and the taxpayer's actions (*Tooth v HMRC* FTT (TC 5452), [2016] UKFTT 723 (TC)).'

10

Capital Allowances on Plant and Machinery

First-year allowances

[10.18] The allowance in list item (c) (low emission or electrically-propelled cars) has now been extended so as to cover qualifying expenditure incurred at any time before 1 April 2021. [*SI 2016 No 984, Arts 2–4*]. See also **10.22** below.

A new list item (f) is added as follows:

'**on and after 23 November 2016 and before 6 April 2019** by any person on **electric charge-point equipment,** unused and not second-hand, installed solely for the purpose of charging electric vehicles, in which case the maximum FYA is **100%.** The legislation will be in *FA 2017* (Autumn Statement, 23 November 2016 at www.gov.uk/government/publications/capital-allowances-first-year-al lowance-for-electric-charge-points).'

Energy-saving plant or machinery

[10.20] A reference is inserted to *SI 2016 No 927*, which gives statutory effect to the revised Energy Technology Product List issued on 7 September 2016.

Environmentally beneficial plant or machinery

[10.21] A reference is inserted to *SI 2016 No 952*, which gives statutory effect to the revised Water Technology List issued on 6 July 2016.

Energy-efficient cars

[10.22] It is noted that the legislation has now been enacted to reduce the emissions limit to 50g/km for expenditure incurred on or after 1 April 2018. [*SI 2016 No 984, Arts 2–4*].

Special rate expenditure

[10.28] Under the sub-heading 'Cars', it is noted that the legislation has now been enacted to reduce the emissions limit to 110g/km for expenditure incurred on or after 1 April 2018. [*SI 2016 No 984, Arts 2, 3, 5*].

13

Certificates of Tax Deposit

Introduction

[13.1] The final paragraph is replaced with the following:

'Rates of interest are given at **13.2–13.4** below. For full details of the Certificates of Tax Deposit scheme, including current interest rates and information on making a deposit, see www.gov.uk/guidance/certificate-of-tax-deposit-scheme.'

14

Charities

Qualifying donations

[14.16] In order to take account of the making and receiving of donations by intermediaries, the text is updated to read as follows:

'A "*qualifying donation*" is a gift to a charity by an individual which meets the following conditions:

(a)   it takes the form of a payment of a sum of money;

(b)   it is not subject to a condition as to repayment;

(c)   it is not deductible under the payroll deduction scheme — see **14.20** below;

(d)   it is not deductible in calculating the donor's income from any source;

(e)   it is not conditional on, or associated with, or part of an arrangement involving, the acquisition of property by the charity, otherwise than by way of gift, from the donor or a person connected with him;

(f)   neither the donor nor any person connected with him (see **19** CONNECTED PERSONS) receives any benefit, in consequence of making it, in excess of specified limits (see **14.17** below); and

(g)   the individual (or, after 5 April 2017, an intermediary representing the individual) gives the charity (or, after 5 April 2017, an intermediary representing the charity) a 'gift aid declaration' in relation to the gift.

A gift to charity is not a qualifying donation if the payment is by way of, or amounts in substance to, a waiver by the individual of entitlement to sums (whether principal or interest) due to him from the charity in respect of an amount advanced to the charity on which social investment income tax relief has been obtained (see **71** SOCIAL INVESTMENT RELIEF).

A "*gift aid declaration*" for the purposes of (g) above is a declaration which is given in the manner prescribed by regulations. It may be made in writing, by SMS text, online (including via social media) or orally (e.g. by telephone). It must contain the donor's name and address, the name of the charity, a description of the gift(s) to which it relates, and a statement that the gift(s) is (are) to be qualifying donations for these purposes. In order for the declaration to have effect, it must have been explained to the donor that he must pay sufficient income tax or capital gains tax to cover the tax deemed to be deducted at source from the donation. A donor can give a single declaration (an enduring declaration) to a charity that, in addition to covering the current gift, also covers future gifts that the donor makes to the charity. A charity must maintain a satisfactory auditable (by HMRC) record of gift aid declarations given to it. A donor may cancel a gift aid declaration by giving oral or written notice to the charity. Similar rules apply after 5 April 2017 in relation to donations by intermediaries. An intermediary cannot give an enduring declaration to a charity but an individual may authorise an intermediary to create gift aid declarations on his behalf for all subsequent donations made in the tax year in question.

For the purpose of (g) above, an *"intermediary"* is a person authorised by an individual to give a gift aid declaration to a charity on his behalf, or a person authorised by a charity to receive a gift aid declaration on its behalf, or a person authorised to perform both those roles. Gifts made by individuals through intermediaries will often be made via digital channels. HMRC have the power to impose penalties of up to £3,000 per tax year if a donor intermediary fails to comply with certain requirements imposed by regulations (see *SI 2016 No 1195, Regs 12–17*). For requirements as to record-keeping by donor intermediaries and the providing of an annual statement by donor intermediaries to donors, see *SI 2016 No 1195, Regs 7, 8*.

[ITA 2007, ss 416, 417, 422, 428; FA 2014, Sch 11 para 11; FA 2015, s 20; FA 2016, s 173; SI 2000 No 2074; SI 2005 No 2790; SI 2016 Nos 1010, 1195].

As regards (f) above, the benefit does not have to be received from the charity to be taken into account (see *St Dunstan's v Major* (Sp C 127), [1997] SSCD 212, in which the saving of inheritance tax by personal representatives as a result of the variation of a will to provide for a donation which would otherwise qualify under these provisions constituted a benefit).

The release of a loan not for consideration and not under seal cannot amount to a gift of money (see *Battle Baptist Church v CIR and Woodham* (Sp C 23), [1995] SSCD 176).'

Small cash donations

[14.19] At the end, under a new sub-heading 'Future developments', a new paragraph is added as follows:

'Amendments are made, with effect for 2017/18 onwards, by *Small Charitable Donations and Childcare Payments Act 2017*. The scheme will now apply to contactless payments made in the UK and not just to cash donations. The scheme will continue not to apply to donations made via SMS text or other mobile donation services or by card donations made online, by telephone or using chip and PIN. The £20 limit per donation will continue, as will the

£8,000 limit. The eligibility conditions at (a) and (b) above are abolished. The special rules for charities running charitable activities in community buildings are amended.'

16

Claims

Claims etc not included in returns

[16.3] A case citation is updated to read as follows: *R (oao De Silva) v HMRC* CA, [2016] STC 1333.

18

Compensation for Loss of Employment (and Damages)

Introduction

[18.1] Under the sub-heading 'Future development', the text is updated to read as follows:

'Legislation amending the income tax treatment of termination payments is to be included in *FA 2017* and will have effect for 2018/19 onwards. The changes will also have a consequential effect on the national insurance treatment of termination payments. Where employers make payments on termination of employment, including all payments in lieu of notice (PILONs) (and not just contractual PILONs), they will be required to identify, using a new statutory formula, the amount of basic pay that the employee would have received if he had worked his full notice period. That amount will be treated as earnings; Class 1 national insurance contributions (NICs) will therefore be payable in respect of them. Those earnings will not qualify for the exemption from income tax on the first £30,000 of termination payments. The Government had intended to make the said formula apply to any expected bonus pay in addition to basic pay, but this proposal has been dropped following consultation. The formula will not apply to statutory redundancy pay.

Any excess of total payments made, and benefits provided, over the amount identified as earnings as described above will be chargeable to income tax to the extent that it is over £30,000. That excess will also be made subject to employer Class 1A NICs.

The foreign service relief at **18.5**(vi) below is to be abolished (other than in the case of seafarers). A new exemption will, however, apply to a termination payment if the employee's relevant earnings in connection with which the payment is received, and any earnings from associated employments, are broadly neither earnings for a tax year for which the employee is UK resident (and thus within **27.4** EMPLOYMENT INCOME) nor UK-based earnings for a tax year for which the employee is non-UK resident (and thus within **27.10** EMPLOYMENT INCOME).

(Autumn tax update, 5 December 2016 at www.gov.uk/government/publicati ons/income-tax-and-national-insurance-contributions-treatment-of-terminati on-payments).'

Compensation for termination of office or employment — general tax law

[18.2] A case citation is updated to read as follows: *Tottenham Hotspur v HMRC* FTT (TC 5143), [2016] UKFTT 389 (TC) [2016] SFTD 803.

Termination payments and benefits — the charge to tax

[18.4] At the end of the first paragraph, a sentence is added as follows:

'The legislation does not allow the chargeable amount to be reduced by reference to share options forfeited on termination of employment (*Sjumarken v HMRC* UT, [2017] STC 239).'

Exceptions from charge

[18.5] At the end of list item (i), a sentence is added as follows:

'Legislation to be included in *FA 2017*, with effect for 2018/19 onwards, will clarify that "injury" does not include injury to feelings, unless it amounts to a psychiatric injury or other recognised medical condition (Autumn tax update, 5 December 2016 at www.gov.uk/government/publications/income-tax-and-n ational-insurance-contributions-treatment-of-termination-payments).'

At the end of list item (vi), a sentence is added as follows:

'See also **18.1** above under Future Development.'

20

Construction Industry Scheme (CIS)

Registration as a sub-contractor

[20.7] Under the sub-heading 'Cancellation of registration', the decision in J P Whitter (Waterwell Engineers) Ltd has been affirmed by the Court of Appeal (*J P Whitter (Waterwell Engineers) Ltd v HMRC* CA 2016, [2017] STC 149).

21

Deceased Estates

Grossing-up of estate income

[21.6] At the end, a new paragraph is added as follows:

'HMRC have clarified that where dividends were received by the estate before 6 April 2016 but are not paid over to the beneficiary until after that date, the beneficiary is deemed to have paid tax at 7.5% (the dividend ordinary rate for 2016/17 onwards) on the grossed-up amount of the dividend. This tax credit will be set against the beneficiary's tax liability on estate income but is a notional tax credit and thus not repayable. As regards dividends received by the estate on or after 6 April 2016 the personal representatives will pay tax on them at 7.5%, and beneficiaries will be entitled to credit for the tax paid. See HMRC Trusts Estates newsletter, December 2016 at www.gov.uk/governmen t/publications/hm-revenue-and-customs-trusts-and-estates-newsletters.'

Absolute interests

[21.7] At the end of note (b) to the Example, a new sentence is added as follows:

'See **21.6** above as to the notional tax credit available to beneficiaries where dividends were received by the estate before 6 April 2016 but are not paid over to the beneficiary until after that date.'

22

Deduction of Tax at Source

Yearly interest

[22.12] After the fourth paragraph, a new paragraph is added as follows:

'Statutory interest paid to creditors in a company administration is *not* yearly interest, even if paid in respect of a period exceeding one year (*Lehman Brothers International (In Administration); Lomas v HMRC* Ch D, [2016] All ER (D) 72 (Oct)).'

Under the sub-heading 'Peer-to-peer loans', the text is updated to read as follows:

'See **64.9** SAVINGS AND INVESTMENT INCOME as to the nature of peer-to-peer (P2P) lending. Whether tax must be deducted from interest paid on a P2P loan will depend on the identity of both lender and borrower. The many-to-many lending model used by the P2P industry means that the application of the yearly interest rule is complex for loans made through P2P platforms and may lead to inconsistent tax treatment. Legislation will be included in *FA 2017*, with effect on and after 6 April 2017, to remove the requirement to deduct tax at source from interest on P2P loans (Autumn tax update, 5 December 2016 at www.gov.uk/government/publications/deduction-of-income-tax-from-savin gs-income). In the meantime interest on P2P loans may be paid *without* deduction of tax. This applies to interest payments made by (i) a UK borrower to a UK P2P platform; (ii) a UK P2P platform to anyone; and (iii) any intermediary to or from a UK P2P platform. In all cases the P2P platform must be authorised by the Financial Conduct Authority (including interim authorisation). (HMRC Brief 2 (2016), 8 January 2016).'

25

Disguised Remuneration

Introduction

[25.1] Under the sub-heading 'Future Developments', the text is updated to read as follows:

'Legislation to be included in *FA 2017*, generally with effect on and after 6 April 2017, will seek to strengthen the disguised remuneration rules. It will incorporate the following measures.

Loans outstanding on 5 April 2019

A person (P) is to be treated as taking a relevant step for the purposes of the disguised remuneration provisions if P has made a loan (or equivalent arrangement — a quasi-loan) to a relevant person (as defined in **25.6** below under Payment of sum, transfer of asset etc.) on or after 6 April 1999 and any part of it remains outstanding immediately before the end of 5 April 2019. For the purpose of ascertaining the value of the relevant step, the step is to be treated as involving a sum of money equal to the amount of the loan outstanding at the time P is treated as taking the step. P is treated as taking the step immediately before the end of 5 April 2019 or, if the loan is an "approved fixed term loan" on 5 April 2019, immediately before the end of the approved repayment date (the date by which, under the terms of the loan, the whole of it must be repaid). A loan is an *"approved fixed term loan"* on 5 April 2019 if it is at that time a qualifying loan (broadly a pre-9 December 2010 loan whose term cannot exceed ten years) which has been approved by HMRC. A person may apply to HMRC in 2018 (or later if HMRC allow in any particular case) for approval of a qualifying loan. HMRC will approve the loan only if they are satisfied that regular repayments have been made (at intervals not exceeding 53 weeks) and that the loan is on commercial terms.

Loan transfers and write-offs/releases of loans

A person will additionally be treated as taking a relevant step within *ITEPA 2003, s 554C* (see **25.6** below under Payment of sum, transfer of asset etc.) if:

(a)   he acquires a right to payment of a sum of money, or to a transfer of assets, where there is a connection between the acquisition of the right and either a payment made, by way of loan or otherwise, to a relevant person or a transfer of assets to a relevant person; or

(b)   he releases or writes off the whole or a part of a loan made to a relevant person or an acquired debt of the kind mentioned in (a).

Close companies' gateway

A new close companies' gateway will be introduced to put beyond doubt when the disguised remuneration provisions apply to remuneration of employees and directors who have a connection to a close company. If the employer is a close company, this gateway must be considered in addition to the basic conditions at **25.2** below. The close companies' gateway will not apply where the payment to the third party that provides the benefits to the employee is a distribution. The legislation will apply where an individual has a qualifying connection with a close company, which includes his being an employee/director (or former employee/director) of the company or having (or having had at any time) a material interest in the company.

Overlap with earlier relevant step

Under Rule 2 in **25.3** below, the value of a relevant step is reduced by the value of any earlier relevant step relating to the same employment (and within the charge to tax under the disguised remuneration provisions) if there is an overlap between the sum of money or asset which is the subject of the relevant steps. See an amendment will be made so that this reduction will be possible only where the liability from the earlier step is paid in full. The only exception will be where, before the later charge arises, either the earlier tax liability is not yet due and payable or the relevant person has reached an agreement with HMRC to pay it.

(Autumn tax update, 5 December 2016 at www.gov.uk/government/publicati ons/tackling-disguised-remuneration-update).'

26

Double Tax Relief

Double tax agreements

[26.2] The following items in the main list of Agreements are added or amended:

Canada (1980/709; 1980/780; 1980/1528; 1985/1996; 1987/2071; 1996/1782; 2000/3330; 2003/2619; 2014/3274 (2014 protocol applies from 6 April 2015 (UK), but from 1 January 2015 as regards taxes withheld at source, and 1 January 2015 (Canada)); 2015/2011 (2015 exchange of notes applies from 21 December 2016 in both territories)),

Guernsey (1952/1215; 1994/3209; 2009/3011; 2015/2008 (applies from 6 April 2016 (UK) and 1 January 2017 (Guernsey)); 2016/750 (2016 exchange of letters applies from 16 March 2016 in both territories)),

Isle of Man (1955/1205; 1991/2880; 1994/3208; 2009/228; 2013/3148; 2016/749 (2016 exchange of letters applies from 16 March 2016 in both territories)),

Jersey (1952/1216; 1994/3210; 2009/3012; 2015/2009 (applies from 6 April 2016 (UK) and 1 January 2017 (Jersey)); 2016/752 (2016 exchange of letters applies from 16 March 2016 in both territories)),

Turkmenistan (2016/1217 (applies from 6 April 2017 (UK), but from 1 January 2017 as regards taxes withheld at source, and 1 January 2017 (Turkmenistan) but from 19 December 2016 in both territories as regards exchange of information)),

United Arab Emirates (2016/754 (applies from 1 January 2017 in both territories)),

Uruguay (2016/753 (applies from 1 January 2017 in both territories)),

The following item is added to the list of Exchange of Information Agreements: **Brazil** (2015/1887 (not yet in force)).

In the Note on USSR, the final sentence is replaced with the following:

'Note the new Agreement between the UK and Turkmenistan. The position for the remaining former Republic (Belarus) with which a new convention is not yet in force remains as before. (HMRC SP 4/01; HMRC Notice, 20 February 2014).'

Special agreement with Switzerland

[26.11] The opening paragraph is replaced with the following:

'On 6 October 2011, the UK Government entered into an agreement with Switzerland to tackle offshore tax evasion. This was subsequently amended by a protocol signed on 20 March 2012. The agreement came into force on 1 January 2013. It covers not only ordinary bank accounts held by individual UK taxpayers in Switzerland but any form of bankable assets booked or deposited with a Swiss paying agent, including cash, precious metals, stocks, options and structured financial products. Safe deposit boxes, real property and chattels are, however, excluded. The agreement also gives HMRC powers to discover whether an individual UK taxpayer has an account in Switzerland. The agreement is given legal effect in the UK by *FA 2012, s 218, Sch 36*, which also set out the effect of the agreement on UK tax liabilities.

The agreement was **terminated** by mutual agreement with effect on and after **1 January 2017**. The UK and Switzerland will instead share information under the Common Reporting Standard (see **34.13** HMRC — ADMINISTRATION).

See www.gov.uk/government/publications/uk-swiss-confederation-taxation-co-operation-agreement.'

Under the sub-heading 'Withholding tax', it is noted that the withholding tax came to an end on 31 December 2016 in line with the termination of the agreement.

27

Employment Income

Salary sacrifice arrangements

[27.15A] New text is added as follows:

'For official guidance on salary sacrifice arrangements see www.gov.uk/guidan ce/salary-sacrifice-and-the-effects-on-paye and HMRC Employment Income Manual EIM42750–42790.

Under legislation to be included in *FA 2017*, where benefits-in-kind are provided via salary sacrifice arrangements, there will be a tax charge on the greater of the salary forgone and the cash equivalent of the benefit. The following benefits will be outside the scope of this measure: employer pension contributions and advice, employer-provided childcare, cycle to work schemes and company cars with emissions not exceeding 75g/km. Otherwise, the measure will have effect for all contracts for benefits-in-kind involving salary sacrifice arrangements entered into on or after 6 April 2017. Employees already in such contracts at that date will become subject to the new rules in respect of those contracts on 6 April 2018 or, in the case of cars, accommodation and school fees, 6 April 2021. If pre-6 April 2017 arrangements are varied or renewed after 6 April 2017, these will be treated for these purposes as new arrangements, and the transitional protection will cease. If, however, a variation is necessary for reasons beyond the employee's control (e.g. a car subject to the arrangements is stolen) or the arrangements are suspended due to statutory leave, this will not trigger the new rules (Autumn tax update, 5 December 2016 at www.gov.uk/government/publications/income-tax-limita tion-of-salary-sacrifice).'

Benefits-in-kind generally

[27.24] After the opening paragraph, a new paragraph is added as follows:

'Whether a person is a member of another's family or household is determined by *ITEPA 2003, s 721(4)(5)*. In *Baylis v HMRC* FTT (TC 5454), [2016] UKFTT 725 (TC), [2017] SFTD 217 it was held that HMRC has no discretion in allocating tax charges to family members (in this case to a father or daughter) and that *section 721(4)* itself provides a hierarchy with "spouse" coming before "'parent".'

List item (e) is updated to read as follows:

'Pension information and advice given to an employee on the employer's behalf where the cash equivalent of the benefit (see **27.29** below) does not in total exceed £150 for the tax year; if there is an excess over £150, the full amount is taxable and not just the excess. This exemption is to be replaced for 2017/18 onwards by an exemption for the first £500 worth of pensions advice provided to an employee, including advice on the general financial and tax issues relating to pensions (see **27.26**(xxxa) below). See also **27.26**(xxx) below.'

Other exceptions from charge

[27.26] At the end of list item (xxviii) (advice relating to proposed employee shareholder agreements), a new paragraph is added as follows:

'The above exemption is to continue notwithstanding the abolition of tax reliefs in connection with shares acquired under employee shareholder agreements (Autumn Statement, 23 November 2016 at www.gov.uk/government/p ublications/income-tax-and-capital-gains-tax-employee-shareholder-status).'

A new list item (xxxa) is added as follows:

'**Pensions advice: general (prospective).** Under legislation to be included in *FA 2017*, with effect for 2017/18 onwards, a new income tax exemption will cover the first £500 worth of pensions advice provided or reimbursed to an employee (or former or prospective employee) in a tax year. It will allow advice not only on pensions, but also on the general financial and tax issues relating to pensions. This will replace the more limited exemption at **27.24**(e) above. The exemption will apply if the advice is made available to employees generally or to employees generally at a particular location. However, it will also be capable of applying when the pensions advice is tailored to the employee's specific personal circumstances of nearing retirement either by age or ill-health (Autumn tax update, 5 December 2016 at www.gov.uk/governm ent/publications/employer-arranged-pensions-advice-exemption).'

List item (xxx) is now headed 'Independent pensions advice in respect of conversions and transfers of benefits', but the text remains unchanged.

Cash equivalent of a benefit

[27.29] After the definition of 'annual value', and under a new sub-heading 'Making good', a new paragraph is added as follows:

'"*Making good*" means giving something (usually a cash payment) to the person providing a benefit-in-kind in return for it. Under legislation to be included in *FA 2017*, with effect for all benefits provided in 2017/18 or subsequent years, a general deadline will be introduced by which employees need to make good any part of the cost of the benefit if a deduction is to be allowed for the amount made good. The deadline will be 6 July following the end of the tax year in question. This will replace pre-existing deadlines relating to cars, vans and fuel but will not apply to voluntarily payrolled benefits, for which see **52.28** PAY AS YOU EARN (Autumn tax update, 5 December 2016 at www.gov.uk/government/publications/dates-for-making-good-on-benefits-in-kind).'

Under the sub-heading 'Apportionment', the text is updated to read as follows:

'Where appropriate, e.g. where an asset is not available for the whole of a tax year or where it is available to more than one person, only a corresponding proportion of the cost etc. of the benefit (determined as above) is brought in. See *ITEPA 2003, s 204*, HMRC Employment Income Manual EIM21200, 21637 and *Kerr v Brown; Boyd v Brown* (Sp C 333, 333A), [2002] SSCD 434, [2003] SSCD 266. Legislation to be included in *FA 2017*, with effect for 2017/18 onwards, will set out more detailed statutory rules (replacing current HMRC guidance) for apportioning the cost of the benefit of an asset made available to an employee without transfer of ownership. A reduction will be available for periods during which an asset is unavailable for private use (including any part of the tax year before the asset is provided to the employee and after it ceases to be so provided) and where an asset is shared by two or more employees (Autumn tax update, 5 December 2016 at www.gov.uk/gov ernment/publications/assets-made-available-to-employees-without-transfer).'

Car fuel for private use

[27.34] It is noted that for 2017/18 the amount to which the appropriate percentage should be applied is £22,600. [*SI 2016 No 1174, Arts 1, 2*].

The Table of advisory fuel rates is updated with the following:

Engine size	Petrol	Diesel	LPG*
1.12.16–28.2.17			
1400 cc or less	11p		7p
1600 cc or less		9p	
1401 cc to 2000 cc	14p		9p
1601 cc to 2000 cc		11p	
Over 2000 cc	21p	13p	13p
1.3.17–31.5.17			
1400 cc or less	11p		7p
1600 cc or less		9p	
1401 cc to 2000 cc	14p		9p
1601 cc to 2000 cc		11p	
Over 2000 cc	22p	13p	14p

* LPG = Liquid Petroleum Gas.

Vans for private use

[27.35] It is noted that for 2017/18 the cash equivalent of the van benefit is £3,230 and the cash equivalent of the benefit of fuel for a van is £610. [*SI 2016 No 1174, Arts 1, 3*].

Cheap loan arrangements

[27.39] It is noted that the official rate of interest is reduced from 3% to 2.5% from 6 April 2017. [*SI 2017 No 305*].

Employee liabilities and indemnity insurance

[27.52] At the end, under a new sub-heading 'Future development', new text is added as follows:

'Under legislation to be included in *FA 2017*, with effect for 2017/18 onwards, the relief will be extended to cover cases where there is no allegation made against the employee. It will thus apply additionally to expenses incurred where an employee:

- gives evidence about a matter related to his employment in his capacity as an employee or where he acted in the performance of the duties of the employment; or
- is under general investigation about a matter related to his employment to determine whether or not there has been wrongdoing.

(Autumn tax update, 5 December 2016 at www.gov.uk/government/publicati ons/tax-relief-employee-liabilities-and-indemnity-insurance.)'

Post-employment deductions

[27.53] The final paragraph is updated to read as follows:

'No tax is charged under *ITEPA 2003, s 403* (see **18.4** COMPENSATION FOR LOSS OF EMPLOYMENT) in respect of any amount paid, or benefit provided, to reimburse the former employee for a payment, which, had he not been reimbursed, would have attracted relief under the above provisions; the same applies as regards amounts paid etc. to the former employee's executors or administrators. [*ITEPA 2003, ss 409, 410*]. Under legislation to be included in *FA 2017*, with effect for 2017/18 onwards, this exemption will be extended so as to also apply where the payment in question is made by the former employer on the former employee's behalf (or on behalf of his executors or administrators) (Autumn tax update, 5 December 2016 at www.gov.uk/gove rnment/publications/tax-relief-employee-liabilities-and-indemnity-insurance).'

Additional charge on properties costing over £75,000

[27.64] It is noted where appropriate that the official rate of interest is reduced from 3% to 2.5% for 2017/18.

Sporting testimonials

[27.76] It has been specified that, for the avoidance of double taxation, the DISGUISED REMUNERATION (25) rules do not apply to a sporting testimonial payment that is within the charge under these provisions (or would be but for the £100,000 exemption). [*SI 2016 No 1250*].

Wages in lieu of notice

[27.96] The reader is referred to **18.1** COMPENSATION FOR LOSS OF EMPLOYMENT for proposed changes to the taxation of payments in lieu of notice (PILONs) for 2018/19 onwards.

28
Enterprise Investment Scheme

Introduction

[28.1] Under the sub-heading 'Informal clearance', the telephone number of the Small Company Enterprise Centre is updated to: 0300 123 1083.

The 'no pre-arranged exits' requirement

[28.38] At the end, under a new sub-heading 'Future development', a new paragraph is added as follows:

'Legislation to be included in *FA 2017*, with effect in relation to shares issued on or after 5 December 2016, will exclude from (a) above any arrangements with a view to any shares in the company being exchanged for, or converted into, shares in that company of a different class (Autumn tax update, 5 December 2016 at www.gov.uk/government/publications/income-tax-strea mlining-the-tax-advantaged-venture-capital-schemes).'

29
Exempt Income

Child Trust Funds

[29.10] It is noted that the annual contribution limit of £4,080 will increase to £4,128 with effect on and after 6 April 2017. [*SI 2017 No 185, Reg 4*].

Under the sub-heading 'Stakeholder accounts', the final sentence is deleted. *SI 2017 No 185, Reg 8* removes the obligation on account providers to apply a 'lifestyling' investment strategy in relation to stakeholder accounts.

Individual Savings Accounts (ISAs)

[29.23] It is confirmed that the annual subscription limit will increase to £20,000 for 2017/18. [*SI 2017 No 186, Reg 5*].

Under the sub-heading 'Help to Buy ISAs', a new paragraph is added as follows:

'Any amount held in a Help to Buy ISA on 5 April 2017 can be transferred to a Lifetime ISA (see below) during 2017/18 without this counting towards the £4,000 Lifetime ISA subscription limit (www.gov.uk/government/publication s/individual-savings-accounts-lifetime-isa/individual-savings-accounts-lifetime -isa).'

Under the sub-heading 'Innovative Finance ISAs', the final sentence is updated to read as follows:

'With effect on and after 1 November 2016, certain company and charity debentures (including debt securities and bonds made available through crowdfunding offers) are eligible for inclusion in an innovative finance ISA. [*SI 2016 No 977*].'

Under the sub-heading 'Lifetime ISAs', the text is updated to read as follows:

'A Lifetime ISA is to be introduced from April 2017 for individuals aged 18 to 39 inclusive. The primary legislation is in *Savings (Government Contributions) Act 2017*. Eligible investors will be able to contribute up to £4,000 per year to a Lifetime ISA, and will receive a Government bonus equal to 25% of their contributions. Contributions to a Lifetime ISA will count towards the overall annual ISA subscription limit. Funds in a Lifetime ISA, including the bonus, can be used to buy a first home (costing up to £450,000) at any time from 12 months after the account is opened, and can be withdrawn from the age of 60. Investors can withdraw their funds at other times, but (except in certain cases of terminal illness) the bonus element plus any interest or growth on that element must then be returned to the Government, and a 5% charge will also be applied; the total amount due will be collected and paid to HMRC by the account manager. No charge or clawback of tax relief will be made in the event of an account holder's death. Any type of investment which qualifies to be held in a cash ISA or stocks and shares ISA will also qualify to be held in a Lifetime ISA. Any amount held in a Help to Buy ISA (see above) on 5 April 2017 can be transferred to a Lifetime ISA during 2017/18 without this counting towards the £4,000 Lifetime ISA subscription limit.

See www.gov.uk/government/publications/individual-savings-accounts-lifetim e-isa/individual-savings-accounts-lifetime-isa.'

Junior ISAs

[29.27] It is noted that the annual subscription limit will increase to £4,128 for 2017/18. [*SI 2017 No 186, Reg 6*].

34

HMRC — Administration

Office of Tax Simplification

[34.9] The final sentence is updated to read as follows:

'*FA 2016* placed the OTS on a permanent, statutory footing from 28 November 2016. [*SI 2016 No 1133*].'

Common Reporting Standard

[34.13] A link is added to www.oecd.org/tax/automatic-exchange/crs-imple mentation-and-assistance/crs-by-jurisdiction, which shows the current state of implementation of all jurisdictions committed to the CRS.

The final paragraph is deleted. Under a new sub-heading 'Client notification requirement', new text is added as follows:

'On and after 30 September 2016, persons who provide professional advice or services in respect of taxation or finance involving overseas income or assets are required to notify their clients about matters including the CRS, the penalties for offshore tax evasion and the opportunities to disclose previous offshore evasion to HMRC. The regulations require a standard notification letter, headed "If you have money or other assets abroad, you could owe tax in the UK", to be sent to affected clients no later than 31 August 2017. Affected clients are those to whom the adviser has provided advice or services about income or assets outside the UK, or who the adviser has referred overseas for such advice or services, but disregarding clients for whom the adviser has completed and submitted a personal tax return reflecting such advice or services. The penalty for non-compliance is £3,000. A similar obligation falls upon financial intermediaries. See www.gov.uk/government/pu blications/client-notification-income-or-assets-abroad for more information, including the text of the standard letter. See also HMRC International Exchange of Information Manual IEIM600000–609000. [*FA 2013, s 222; F(No 2)A 2015, s 50; SI 2015 No 878, Regs 12A–12F, 13, Sch 3; SI 2016 No 899*].'

35

HMRC — Confidentiality of Information

Introduction

[35.1] A new paragraph is added as follows:

'One of the exceptions to the confidentiality rule is that it does not apply to a disclosure made for the purposes of a function of HMRC. [*Commissioners for Revenue and Customs Act 2005, s 18(2)(a)(i)*]. In *R (oao Ingenious Media Holdings plc) v HMRC* SC, [2016] STC 2306, it was held by the SC that the disclosure in question was not justified by this exception; a desire to foster good relations with the media or to publicise HMRC's views about tax avoidance schemes could not possibly justify an official of HMRC discussing the affairs of individual taxpayers with journalists.'

36

HMRC Explanatory Publications

HMRC explanatory leaflets

[36.1] The following entries are added, deleted (where stated) or updated.

CC/FS17	Higher Penalties for Offshore Matters. See www.gov.uk/government/p ublications/compliance-checks-penalties-for-income-tax-and-capital-ga ins-tax-for-offshore-matters-ccfs17.
CC/FS30b	Tax Avoidance Schemes — Penalties for Partnership Follower Notices. See www.gov.uk/government/publications/compliance-checks-tax-avoi dance-schemes-penalties-for-partnership-follower-notices-ccfs30b.
CC/FS34	General Anti-Abuse Rule and Provisional Counteraction Notices. See www.gov.uk/government/publications/compliance-checks-general-anti -abuse-rule-and-provisional-counteraction-notices-ccfs34.
CC/FS38	Serial Tax Avoidance — Warning Notices. See www.gov.uk/governme nt/publications/compliance-checks-serial-tax-avoidance-warning-notic es-ccfs38.
ES/FS1	Deleted
ES/FS2	Deleted
E24	Tips, Gratuities, Service Charges and Troncs (2015) (available at www.gov.uk/government/uploads/system/uploads/attachment_data/fil e/430329/E24_2015_v1_0.pdf).
FEU 50	A Guide to Paying Foreign Entertainers (available at www.gov.uk/gui dance/pay-tax-on-payments-to-foreign-performers).
FFC1	Deleted
FFC1(S)	Deleted

38

HMRC Investigatory Powers

Data-gathering powers

[38.15] A new list item (36) is added to the (1) to (35) list as follows:

'(Prospectively from the date of Royal Assent to *FA 2017* but in relation to relevant data with a bearing on any period whether before, on or after that date) a money service business (other than a bank), i.e. a business providing money transfer, cheque cashing and currency exchange services (Autumn tax update, 5 December 2016 at www.gov.uk/government/publications/data-from -money-service-businesses).'

43

Life Assurance Policies

Partial surrenders and partial assignments

[43.13] At the end, under a new sub-heading 'Future development', a new paragraph is added as follows:

'Legislation to be included in *FA 2017*, with effect on and after 6 April 2017, will assist individuals who, in certain unusual circumstances, have part surrendered or part assigned their policies or contracts and inadvertently triggered taxable gains far in excess of the policy's underlying economic gain. They will be able to apply to HMRC to have the charge recalculated on a just and reasonable basis if HMRC agree that the gain is wholly disproportionate. HMRC expect this measure to affect fewer than ten policy holders per year (Autumn tax update, 5 December 2016 at www.gov.uk/government/publicati ons/part-surrenders-and-part-assignments-of-life-insurance-policies).'

44

Losses

Losses on shares in unlisted trading companies

[44.23] At the end, a new paragraph is added as follows:

'For two more or less concurrent cases involving whether or not shares had been subscribed for and producing different results, see *Murray-Hession v HMRC* FTT (TC 5348), [2016] UKFTT 612 (TC) (taxpayer's appeal allowed) and *Alberg v HMRC* FTT (TC 5357), [2016] UKFTT 621 (TC) (tax-payer's appeal dismissed).'

Employment losses

[44.31] At the end of the third paragraph, a new sentence is added as follows:

'For HMRC's guidance on negative taxable earnings, including examples and reference to *Martin v HMRC*, see HMRC Employment Income Manual EIM00800–00845.'

48

Miscellaneous Income

Theatrical angels

[48.6] The final sentence is replaced with a new paragraph as follows:

'This concession is withdrawn from 31 March 2017. Alongside the concession, a practice had become established whereby profits due to angels were treated as a deductible expense of the production rather than a distribution of profits. This practice is also withdrawn for all new productions from 1 April 2017. Productions using the practice before that date may continue to use it until 31 March 2019. Affected productions were asked to notify HMRC by 31 December 2016 of their intention to take advantage of this (www.gov.uk/government/publications/withdrawal-of-extra-statutory-concession-esc-a94-t heatre-angels).'

Income not otherwise charged

[48.7] After the second paragraph, a new paragraph is added as follows:

'See 75.2A TRADING INCOME for the relief to be introduced for 2017/18 onwards for small amounts of income otherwise within the above charge.'

50

Offshore Funds

Reporting funds

[50.13] At the end of the third paragraph, a reference is inserted to *SI 2017 No 240*. UK taxpayers with investments in offshore reporting funds pay income tax on their share of a fund's reportable income and capital gains tax on any gains when they dispose of their shares or units. *SI 2017 No 240* has effect for reporting periods beginning on or after 1 April 2017, and stipulates that performance fees charged by investment managers are no longer deductible in computing reportable income. They will instead be available to reduce any gain on disposal.

51

Partnerships

Nature of partnership

[51.2] In the first sentence, a recent decision is cited as follows: *Ashton v HMRC* FTT (TC 5456), [2016] UKFTT 727 (TC).

52

Pay As You Earn

Payments by intermediaries

[52.7] A link is provided to official guidance at www.gov.uk/guidance/empl oyment-status-employment-intermediaries.

Under-deductions

[52.17] The penultimate paragraph is updated, to take account of *West v HMRC*, as follows:

'See also *Bernard & Shaw Ltd v Shaw* KB 1951, 30 ATC 187, and for wilful failure by employer to deduct correct tax, *R v CIR (ex p Chisholm)* QB 1981, 54 TC 722, *R v CIR (ex p Sims)* QB 1987, 60 TC 398 and *R v CIR (ex p Cook)* QB 1987, 60 TC 405. In *R v CIR (ex p McVeigh)* QB 1996, 68 TC 121, accounting entries purporting to deduct tax, where tax not paid over to HMRC, were held not to constitute deduction of tax for these purposes, but see also *West v HMRC* FTT (TC 5285), [2016] UKFTT 536 (TC). In *Blanche v HMRC* FTT (TC 1697), [2011] UKFTT 863 (TC), the employer was held not to have taken reasonable care; therefore the under-deducted tax was not recoverable from the employee.'

PAYE settlement agreements

[52.25] At the end, a new paragraph is added as follows:

'Legislation is to be included in *FA 2017* to simplify the PAYE settlement agreement process for 2018/19 onwards (Autumn tax update, 5 December 2016 at www.gov.uk/government/publications/income-tax-simplifying-the-pa ye-settlement-agreement-process).'

Benefits-in-kind

[52.28] Under the sub-heading 'Voluntary payrolling for 2016/17 onwards', the text is updated to read as follows:

'The PAYE regulations have been amended under powers conferred by *FA 2015, s 17* (and extended by *FA 2016, s 15*) to provide for voluntary payrolling of benefits-in-kind for 2016/17 onwards. Where authorised to do so by HMRC, employers are able to opt to payroll benefits such as cars, car fuel, medical insurance and gym membership (but not living accommodation or cheap loans). For 2017/18 onwards, non-cash vouchers and credit tokens are added to the list of benefits that may be payrolled. Where employers payroll benefits, they do not have to make a return on form P11D (see **52.21** above) for these benefits. Instead, they report the value of the benefits through Real Time Information (see **52.22** above), and the value counts as PAYE income liable to PAYE deductions. The employer can choose which benefits to include.

The cash equivalent of the benefit is computed under the normal rules in 27 EMPLOYMENT INCOME and is then divided by the number of PAYE payments to be made to the employee in the tax year. The resulting amount is the taxable amount of the benefit on which PAYE must be operated. The employer must add that amount to each payment when made. There is provision for in-year adjustment, for example on a change to the benefit provided. Where an employer requires an employee to make good within the tax year any amount of a benefit, the employer can take that into account when calculating the taxable benefit subject to PAYE deductions, but any failure to make good must also be accounted for; in the case of car and van fuel, and credit tokens for 2017/18 onwards, the deadline for making good is extended to 1 June following the tax year. Before 1 June following a tax year, an employer must provide a statement to each affected employee detailing the benefits that were payrolled in the tax year and their cash equivalents. [SI 2003 No 2682, Regs 61A–61M; SI 2015 No 1927, Regs 1, 6; SI 2016 No 1137, Regs 1–9].

For official guidance on voluntary payrolling, including the registration and deregistration process referred to below, see www.gov.uk/guidance/payrolling -tax-employees-benefits-and-expenses-through-your-payroll.'

Registration

'Employers wishing to payroll benefits for the first time have to register online with HMRC before the start of the tax year for which they wish to begin. Registration then continues unless the employer chooses to stop payrolling those benefits, in which case he must deregister online before the start of the tax year for which it is to have effect; it is not possible for a continuing business to cease payrolling benefits during a tax year. Some employers may have had a pre-existing informal payrolling arrangement with HMRC, but this will have automatically come to an end on 5 April 2016.'

54

Penalties

Notification of chargeability: penalties for non-compliance

[54.3] Under the sub-heading 'Reduction for disclosure', the text is revised to read as follows:

'A reduction in a penalty will be given where the taxpayer discloses a failure to notify. The penalty will be reduced to a percentage which reflects the quality of the disclosure and the amount of the reduction will depend on whether the disclosure is "prompted" or "unprompted". A disclosure is *"unprompted"* if made when the taxpayer has no reason to believe HMRC have discovered or are about to discover the failure. In all other cases, disclosures are *"prompted"*.

A person is treated as making a disclosure for these purposes only if he tells HMRC about the failure, he gives them reasonable help in quantifying the tax unpaid and allows them access to records for the purpose of checking how much tax is unpaid.

The penalty cannot be reduced below a minimum percentage as shown in the table below. Where alternate percentages are shown, the higher percentage applies where HMRC do not become aware of the failure until twelve months or more after the time tax first becomes unpaid by reason of the failure, and the lower percentage applies in all other cases.

Standard percentage	Minimum percentage for prompted disclosure	Minimum percentage for unprompted disclosure
30%	10% or 20%	0% or 10%
70%	35%	20%
100%	50%	30%'

Notification of chargeability: penalties for non-compliance — offshore matters and transfers

[54.4] Under the sub-heading 'Reduction for disclosure', the text is updated to read as follows:

'A reduction in a penalty will be given where the taxpayer discloses a failure to notify. The penalty will be reduced to a percentage which reflects the quality of the disclosure and the amount of the reduction will depend on whether the disclosure is "prompted" or "unprompted". A disclosure is "*unprompted*" if made when the taxpayer has no reason to believe HMRC have discovered or are about to discover the failure. In all other cases, disclosures are "*prompted*".

In the case of a *non-deliberate* failure involving an offshore matter, a person is treated as making a disclosure for these purposes only if he tells HMRC about the failure, gives them reasonable help in quantifying the tax unpaid and allows them access to records for the purpose of checking how much tax is unpaid.

In the case of a *deliberate* failure (whether or not concealed) involving an *offshore matter* or any failure involving an *offshore transfer*, a person (P) will be treated as making a disclosure only if P tells HMRC about the failure, gives them reasonable help in quantifying the tax unpaid, and allows them access to records for the purpose of checking how much tax is unpaid. With effect on and after 1 April 2017, P must also tell HMRC if there is:

• any person who encouraged, assisted or otherwise facilitated the failure; and
• any asset situated or held outside the UK that is held on P's behalf by another person,

and must provide further specified details if either is the case.

For a failure involving an offshore matter or offshore transfer the penalty cannot be reduced below a minimum percentage as shown in the table below. The minimum percentage shown in each case applies on and after 1 April 2017 and has effect in relation to 2016/17 onwards; the percentage shown in parentheses immediately after it is the one previously applicable. Where alternate percentages are shown, the higher percentage applies where HMRC do not become aware of the failure until twelve months or more after the time tax first becomes unpaid by reason of the failure, and the lower percentage applies in all other cases.

Standard percentage	Minimum percentage for prompted disclosure	Minimum percentage for unprompted disclosure
30%	10% (10%) or 20% (20%)	0% (0%) or 10% (10%)
45%	15% (15%) or 30% (30%)	0% (0%) or 15% (15%)
60%	20% (20%) or 40% (40%)	0% (0%) or 20% (20%)
70%	45% (35%)	30% (20%)
100%	60% (50%)	40% (30%)
105%	62.5% (52.5%)	40% (30%)
140%	80% (70%)	50% (40%)
150%	85% (75%)	55% (45%)
200%	110% (100%)	70% (60%)'

At the end, under the sub-heading 'Future developments', the text is updated to read as follows:

'With effect on and after a day to be appointed by the Treasury, a new category (category 0) is to be introduced alongside categories 1 to 3 above. A category 0 territory will be a territory designated as such by Treasury order. The intention is that only territories that adopt automatic exchange of information under the Common Reporting Standard (see **34.13** HMRC — ADMINISTRATION) will be given category 0 status.

Category 0 will have the same penalty levels as the current category 1 (and all penalties for domestic matters will be moved to category 0). The current penalty levels for category 1 will be increased from 100%, 70% and 30% to 125%, 87.5% and 37.5% respectively. There will continue to be reductions for prompted and unprompted disclosures. The penalty levels for categories 2 and 3 will remain the same.

[FA 2008, s 123, Sch 41 paras 6, 6A, 6AA, 6AB, 12, 13, 13A, 14; FA 2015, s 120, Sch 20 paras 9–13; FA 2016, s 163, Sch 21 paras 5–8; SI 2011 No 976; SI 2013 No 1618; SI 2016 No 456, Art 4; SI 2017 Nos 259, 345].'

Late filing penalty

[54.5] In the third paragraph under the sub-heading 'Daily penalty', the citation is updated to: *Donaldson v HMRC* CA, [2016] STC 2511.

Under the sub-heading 'Reduction for disclosure', the text is updated to read as follows:

'A reduction in the second tax-geared penalty will be given where the taxpayer discloses information that he was withholding by virtue of his failure to make a return. The penalty will be reduced to a percentage which reflects the quality of the disclosure (including its timing, nature and extent); the amount of the reduction will depend on whether the disclosure is "prompted" or "un-prompted", but cannot be reduced below a minimum percentage as shown in the tables below. The penalty cannot in any case be reduced below £300.

Information involving a domestic matter

Standard percentage	Minimum percentage for prompted disclosure	Minimum percentage for unprompted disclosure
70%	35%	20%
100%	50%	30%

In the case of information involving an offshore matter or offshore transfer, the minimum percentage shown in the table below in each case applies on and after 1 April 2017 and has effect in relation to 2016/17 onwards; the percentage shown in parentheses immediately after it is the one previously applicable.

Information involving an offshore matter or offshore transfer

Standard percentage	Minimum percentage for prompted disclosure	Minimum percentage for unprompted disclosure
70%	45% (35%)	30% (20%)
100%	60% (50%)	40% (30%)
105%	62.5% (52.5%)	40% (30%)
140%	80% (70%)	50% (40%)
150%	85% (75%)	55% (45%)
200%	110% (100%)	70% (60%)

A person (P) is treated as making a disclosure for these purposes only if P tells HMRC about the information, gives them reasonable help in quantifying the tax unpaid by reason of the information having been withheld and allows them access to records for the purpose of quantifying how much tax is unpaid. Where the information disclosed involves an offshore matter or an offshore transfer, then with effect on and after 1 April 2017, P must also tell HMRC if there is:

- any person who encouraged, assisted or otherwise facilitated the withholding of the information; and
- any asset situated or held outside the UK that is held on P's behalf by another person,

and must provide further specified details if either is the case.

A disclosure is *"unprompted"* if made when the taxpayer has no reason to believe HMRC have discovered, or are about to discover, the information. In all other cases, disclosures are *"prompted"."*

At the end, under the sub-heading 'Future developments', the text is updated to read as follows:

'With effect on and after a day to be appointed by the Treasury, a new category (category 0) is to be introduced for the second tax-geared penalty alongside categories 1 to 3 above. A category 0 territory will be a territory designated as such by Treasury order. The intention is that only territories that adopt automatic exchange of information under the Common Reporting Standard (see **34.13** HMRC — ADMINISTRATION) will be given category 0 status.

Category 0 will have the same penalty levels as the current category 1 (and all penalties for domestic matters will be moved to category 0). The higher current penalty levels for category 1 will be increased from 100% and 70% to 125% and 87.5% respectively, with the 5% level staying unchanged. Where both the first and second tax-geared penalties are due in relation to the same tax liability, the total of those penalties will not be able to exceed the new 125% limit. There will continue to be reductions for prompted and unprompted disclosures. The penalty levels for categories 2 and 3 will remain the same.

[FA 2009, s 106, Sch 55 paras 1–6, 6A, 6AA, 6AB,14, 15, 15A, 16, 17, 17A, 17B, 23–27; FA 2013, Sch 50 paras 3–5, 16(2), Sch 51 paras 8, 9; FA 2014, Sch 33 para 5; FA 2015, s 120, Sch 20 paras 14–19; FA 2016, ss 163, 169(6)(7), Sch 21 paras 9–12, Sch 22 para 20(5); SI 2011 No 976; SI 2013 No 1618; SI 2016 No 456, Art 5; SI 2017 Nos 259, 345].'

Careless or deliberate errors in documents

[54.6] At the end, under a new sub-heading 'Future developments', a new paragraph is added as follows:

'Under legislation to be included in *FA 2017*, with effect in relation to documents for tax periods which begin on or after 6 April 2017 and end on or after the date of Royal Assent, there will be a presumption in cases of tax avoidance arrangements defeated by HMRC that a person has failed to take reasonable care. The onus will be on the taxpayer to prove otherwise. The legislation will explicitly describe things that do not amount to taking reasonable care in such cases, e.g. advice given by an interested party or addressed to someone other than the taxpayer or given by a person without the necessary expertise or given without reference to the taxpayer's individual circumstances (Autumn tax update, 5 December 2016 at www.gov.uk/govern ment/publications/strengthening-sanctions-and-deterrents-for-tax-avoidance).'

Amount of penalties

[54.7] Under the sub-heading 'Reduction for disclosure', the text is revised to read as follows:

'A reduction in a penalty will be given where a person discloses an inaccuracy in a document or, in relation to the penalty payable by T, a supply of false information or a withholding of information. The penalty will be reduced to a percentage which reflects the quality of the disclosure and the amount of the reduction will depend on whether the disclosure is "prompted" or "un-prompted".

The penalty cannot be reduced below a minimum percentage as shown in the table below.

Standard percentage	Minimum percentage for prompted disclosure	Minimum percentage for unprompted disclosure
30%	15%	0%
70%	35%	20%
100%	50%	30%

A person is treated as making a disclosure for these purposes only if he tells HMRC about the inaccuracy etc., gives HMRC reasonable help in quantifying the inaccuracy etc. and allows them access to records for the purpose of ensuring that the inaccuracy etc. is fully corrected. A disclosure is '*un-prompted*' if made when the taxpayer has no reason to believe HMRC have discovered, or are about to discover, the inaccuracy etc. In all other cases, disclosures are *"prompted".*'

Amount of penalties — offshore matters and transfers

[54.8] Under the sub-heading 'Reduction for disclosure', the text is updated to read as follows:

'A reduction in a penalty will be given where a person discloses an inaccuracy in a document or, in relation to the penalty payable by T in **54.6** above, a supply of false information or a withholding of information. The penalty will be reduced to a percentage which reflects the quality of the disclosure and the amount of the reduction will depend on whether the disclosure is "prompted" or "unprompted".

A person (X) is treated as making a disclosure for these purposes only if X tells HMRC about the inaccuracy etc., gives HMRC reasonable help in quantifying the inaccuracy etc. and allows them access to records for the purpose of ensuring that the inaccuracy etc. is fully corrected. With effect on and after 1 April 2017, X must also tell HMRC if there is:

• any person who encouraged, assisted or otherwise facilitated the inaccuracy etc.; and

- any asset situated or held outside the UK that is held on X's behalf by another person,

and must provide further specified details if either is the case.

A disclosure is *"unprompted"* if made when the taxpayer has no reason to believe HMRC have discovered, or are about to discover, the inaccuracy etc. In all other cases, disclosures are *"prompted"*.

For an inaccuracy involving an offshore matter or offshore transfer the penalty cannot be reduced below a minimum percentage as shown in the table below. The minimum percentage shown in the table in each case applies on and after 1 April 2017 and has effect in relation to 2016/17 onwards; the percentage shown in parentheses immediately after it is the one previously applicable.

Standard percentage	Minimum percentage for prompted disclosure	Minimum percentage for unprompted disclosure
30%	15% (15%)	0% (0%)
45%	22.5% (22.5%)	0% (0%)
60%	30% (30%)	0% (0%)
70%	45% (35%)	30% (20%)
100%	60% (50%)	40% (30%)
105%	62.5% (52.5%)	40% (30%)
140%	80% (70%)	50% (40%)
150%	85% (75%)	55% (45%)
200%	110% (100%)	70% (60%)'

Under the sub-heading 'Future developments', the text is updated to read as follows:

'With effect on and after a day to be appointed by the Treasury, a new category (category 0) is to be introduced alongside categories 1 to 3 above. A category 0 territory will be a territory designated as such by Treasury order. The intention is that only territories that adopt automatic exchange of information under the Common Reporting Standard (see **34.13** HMRC — ADMINISTRATION) will be given category 0 status.

Category 0 will have the same penalty levels as the current category 1 (and all penalties for domestic matters will be moved to category 0). The current penalty levels for category 1 will be increased from 30%, 70% and 100% to 37.5%, 87.5% and 125% respectively. There will continue to be reductions for prompted and unprompted disclosures. The penalty levels for categories 2 and 3 will remain the same.

Where penalties are imposed on P and T (in **54.6** above) in respect of the same inaccuracy, the aggregate penalty will not be able to exceed 100% of the potential lost revenue for an inaccuracy in new category 0 or 125% of the potential lost revenue for an inaccuracy in amended category 1.

[*FA 2007, Sch 24 paras 4, 4A, 4AA, 10A, 12(4)(5), 21A, 21B, 23B; FA 2012, s 219; FA 2015, s 120, Sch 20 paras 2–8; FA 2016, s 163, Sch 21 paras 1–4; SI 2011 No 976; SI 2013 No 1618; SI 2016 No 456, Art 3; SI 2017 Nos 259, 345*].'

Offshore tax evasion

[54.9] At the end, under a new sub-heading 'Client notification requirement', a new paragraph is added as follows:

'On and after 30 September 2016, persons who provide professional advice or services in respect of taxation or finance involving overseas income or assets are required to notify their clients about matters including the Common Reporting Standard (see **34.13** HMRC — ADMINISTRATION), the penalties for offshore tax evasion and the opportunities to disclose previous offshore evasion to HMRC. The regulations require a standard notification letter, headed 'If you have money or other assets abroad, you could owe tax in the UK', to be sent to affected clients no later than 31 August 2017. Affected clients are those to whom the adviser has provided advice or services about income or assets outside the UK, or who the adviser has referred overseas for such advice or services, but disregarding clients for whom the adviser has completed and submitted a personal tax return reflecting such advice or services. The penalty for non-compliance is £3,000. A similar obligation falls upon financial intermediaries. See www.gov.uk/government/publications/client-notification-income-or-assets-abroad for more information, including the text of the standard letter. [*FA 2013, s 222; F(No 2)A 2015, s 50; SI 2015 No 878, Regs 12A–12F, 13, Sch 3; SI 2016 No 899*].'

After the above addition, under a further new sub-heading 'Failure to correct', new text is added as follows:

'Legislation to be included in *FA 2017* will introduce a new requirement for those who have failed to declare past (pre–6 April 2017) UK tax liabilities on offshore interests to correct that situation by disclosing the relevant information to HMRC. For example, a taxpayer who submitted an inaccurate return by omitting a source of offshore income will be required to provide sufficient information to HMRC to allow the inaccuracy to be corrected and the under-declared tax to be assessed and paid. The window for correction to be made will be open from date of Royal Assent until 30 September 2018. Those who have failed to correct before 1 October 2018 will then be liable to a penalty. The measure applies in relation to failure to notify chargeability to tax, failure to deliver a return or inaccuracy in a document, in each case where there is an offshore element.

The penalty for failure to correct (FTC) will be a maximum of 200% of the potential lost revenue relating to the offshore tax non-compliance that has not been corrected. HMRC may reduce the penalty to reflect the quality of the taxpayer's disclosure, but not below 100%. The asset-based penalty at **54.11** below will also be applied, as will the penalty at **54.10** below if assets or funds have been moved in an attempt to avoid the requirement to correct. There will be a reasonable excuse let-out. HMRC will be able to publish information about a person who incurs one or more FTC penalties involving potential lost revenue in excess of £25,000, or five or more FTC penalties of any kind.

(Autumn tax update, 5 December 2016 at www.gov.uk/government/publicati ons/tackling-offshore-tax-evasion-requirement-to-correct.)

It is anticipated that in most cases the requirement to correct will be met via HMRC's Worldwide Disclosure Facility at www.gov.uk/guidance/worldwide-disclosure-facility-make-a-disclosure. The Facility launched on 5 September 2016 and is available to anyone disclosing a UK tax liability that relates wholly or partly to an offshore issue. See www.gov.uk/guidance/offshore-disclosure-f acilities.'

Asset-based penalty for offshore inaccuracies and failures

[54.11] It is noted that the rules described here have effect on and after 1 April 2017 in relation to 2016/17 onwards. [*SI 2017 No 277*].

Enabling offshore evasion

[54.19] It is noted that the rules described here have effect on and after 1 January 2017. [*SI 2016 No 1249*].

Enabling tax avoidance

[54.19A] New text is added as follows:

'*FA 2017* will introduce a new penalty for individuals or entities ("enablers") who enable the use of abusive tax arrangements which HMRC later defeat. The penalty will apply to steps taken by enablers after Royal Assent to *FA 2017*. It is designed to penalise those who design, market or otherwise facilitate avoidance arrangements and not those who simply advise, report or otherwise provide an opinion on such arrangements and whose advice does not result in any changes thereto. Anyone unwittingly becoming involved in arrangements will be excluded. Arrangements will be treated as abusive if they meet a "double reasonableness test". This is so that the penalty does not inhibit genuine commercial transactions. External scrutiny will be provided by the GAAR Advisory Panel (see **4.3** ANTI-AVOIDANCE). The amount of the penalty will be equal to the consideration received by the enabler for anything done to enable the arrangements. HMRC will be able to publish information about an enabler liable to penalties exceeding a specified amount (Autumn tax update, 5 December 2016 at www.gov.uk/government/publications/strengthening-san ctions-and-deterrents-for-tax-avoidance).'

Publishing details of deliberate tax defaulters

[54.34] It is noted that the rules described in the final paragraph have effect on and after 1 April 2017. [*SI 2017 No 261*].

55

Pension Income

Taxable pension income

[55.2] At the end, under a new sub-heading 'Future developments', a new paragraph is added as follows:

'Under legislation to be included in *FA 2017*, with effect for 2017/18 onwards, foreign pensions and lump sums will be taxed to the same extent as those paid from a registered pension scheme. The 10% deduction for foreign pensions will be abolished, bringing 100%, instead of 90%, of foreign pension income into the charge to UK tax (Autumn tax update, 5 December 2016 at www.gov.uk/government/publications/foreign-pension-schemes).'

56

Pension Provision

Regulations

[56.10] At the end, a new paragraph is added as follows:

'*The Registered Pension Schemes (Bridging Pensions) and Appointed Day Regulations 2016 (SI 2016 No 1005)* seek to ensure that pre-existing circumstances when a bridging pension can be reduced without breaching the rules to be a scheme pension are maintained following the introduction of a single-tier State pension on 6 April 2016. The regulations have effect in relation to reductions in payments of scheme pensions made on or after that date. A bridging pension is a higher level of scheme pension that may be paid between retirement and attainment of State pension age.'

Annual allowance

[56.23] Under the sub-heading 'Money purchase annual allowance', a new paragraph is added as follows:

'Subject to consultation the Government intends to reduce the money purchase annual allowance from £10,000 to £4,000 for 2017/18 onwards (Autumn Statement, 23 November 2016 at www.gov.uk/government/consultations/reducing-the-money-purchase-annual-allowance).'

A reference is inserted to *SI 2017 No 11, Regs 1, 4, 5*. This instrument amends *Registered Pension Schemes (Provision of Information) Regulations 2006 (SI 2006 No 567)*. It sets out the information that the scheme administrator of a registered pension scheme must provide when specified lump sum death benefits are paid on or after 6 April 2016 to the trustees of a trust. It also sets out the information that the trustees who have received these payments must provide when making a payment out of those funds to a beneficiary of the trust.

Special rules for 2015/16

[56.25] A reference is inserted to *SI 2017 No 11, Regs 1, 4.* This makes minor technical changes to *SI 2006 No 567, Reg 14A(1A).*

Other tax charges

[56.27] At the end of the penultimate paragraph of list item (b) (special lump sum death benefits charge), new text is added as follows:

'Regulations provide for the provision of necessary information by the scheme administrator to the trustees and by the trustees to the beneficiary. [*SI 2006 No 567, Regs 10A, 10B; SI 2017 No 11, Regs 1, 3*].'

Overseas pension schemes — tax charges

[56.29] Under the sub-heading 'Other tax charges', the paragraph immediately below the (a) to (c) list is updated to read as follows:

'The charges listed above similarly apply in relation to payments made to or in respect of a member of a non-UK scheme at a time when he is non-UK resident, provided he has been UK resident at some time earlier in the tax year in which the payment is made or at some time in the five preceding tax years. Under legislation to be included in *FA 2017*, the last-mentioned period is to be extended to the ten preceding tax years insofar as the payment is referable to so much of the member's UK pension fund as represents tax-relieved contributions, or tax-exempt provision, made on or after 6 April 2017 (Autumn tax update, 5 December 2016 at www.gov.uk/government/publications/foreign-p ension-schemes).'

Taxable property

[56.32] At the end of the paragraph beginning "Tangible moveable property" has its general meaning and will include', a new sentence is added as follows:

'Printing presses have been held to be tangible moveable property (*Morgan Lloyd Trustees Ltd (as administrator of the Wren Press Pension Scheme) v HMRC* FTT (TC 5625), [2017] UKFTT 131 (TC)).'

Employer-financed retirement benefits schemes: definitions

[56.35] At the end of the bulleted list of excluded benefits, a new list item is added as follows:

'(For 2016/17 onwards) "trivial benefits" provided to the former employee or a member of his family or household. *"Trivial benefits"* are low value benefits that would have been trivial benefits within **27.25** EMPLOYMENT INCOME if they had been provided in the course of the employee's employment. If the former employer is a close company when the benefit is provided, and the former employee was a director or other office-holder at any time when the former employer was a close company (or is a member of the family or household of such a director etc.), the £300 annual cap in **27.25** applies. [*SI 2016 No 1036*].'

Other pension funds

[56.40] At the end, new text is added as follows:

'Under legislation to be included in *FA 2017*, with effect for 2017/18 onwards, it will no longer be possible to establish new pension schemes under *ICTA 1988, s 615* or to make contributions to pre-existing schemes. Annuities out of funds accrued in a *section 615* scheme before 6 April 2017 will still be covered by the above rules (Autumn tax update, 5 December 2016 at www.gov.uk/g overnment/publications/foreign-pension-schemes).'

57

Personal Service Companies etc (IR35)

Introduction

[57.1] Under the sub-heading 'Future development', the text is updated to read as follows:

'Under legislation to be included in *FA 2017*, with effect for payments made to intermediaries on or after 6 April 2017 (including payments under contracts made before that date), where an intermediary provides the services of a worker to a public sector body, such as a Government department, NHS trust or local authority, the responsibility for determining whether or not the IR35 rules apply, operating those rules where they do apply and deducting any tax and NICs due will shift from the intermediary to the public sector body (or, where applicable, the recruiting agency through which the public sector body engages). The 5% deduction at **57.8** below will *not* be available in these circumstances (Autumn tax update, 5 December 2016 at www.gov.uk/govern ment/publications/off-payroll-working-in-the-public-sector-reform-of-the-inte rmediaries-legislation). See also the technical note at www.gov.uk/governmen t/publications/off-payroll-working-in-the-public-sector-reform-of-the-interme diaries-legislation-technical-note.'

59

Property Income

Introduction

[59.1] Under the sub-heading 'Future development', the text is updated to read as follows:

'Legislation to be included in *FA 2017* will introduce a £1,000 allowance for property income for 2017/18 onwards. The new allowance will mean that individuals with property income of £1,000 or less will no longer need to declare or pay tax on that income. See 59.4A below.

Also for 2017/18 onwards, optional use of the cash basis for smaller businesses will be extended to property businesses. See 59.4B below.'

Relief for small amounts of income

[59.4A] New text is added as follows:

'Legislation to be included in *FA 2017* will introduce two separate £1,000 allowances for property income and trading income. The allowances will first have effect by reference to income for 2017/18. They will not apply to property businesses carried on in partnership or where rent-a-room relief is available (see 59.14 below). See also 75.2A TRADING INCOME.

Each of the two allowances operates as follows. Where the individual's gross receipts (i.e. before deducting expenses) do not exceed the £1,000 limit, there is no charge to tax. The individual can, however, elect that this should not apply. Where gross receipts exceed the limit, the individual can elect to use an alternative method of calculating the taxable income. Under this method the charge to tax is on gross receipts less £1,000. Once full relief has been given, or the alternative method applied, there is no tax relief for the expenses that would otherwise have been deductible from receipts in computing taxable income. Under the alternative method, it is for the individual to decide how a £1,000 deduction should be split between two or more trades or property businesses.

Elections must be made by the first anniversary of 31 January following the tax year and have effect only for the tax year for which they are made. There will be an anti-avoidance rule to prevent employers reclassifying payments to employees (or to persons connected with employees) so as to bring those payments within these allowances.

(Autumn tax update, 5 December 2016 at www.gov.uk/government/publicati ons/income-tax-new-tax-allowance-for-property-and-trading-income.)'

Cash basis for smaller property businesses

[59.4B] New text is added as follows:

'For 2017/18 onwards, the optional use of the cash basis will be extended to eligible property businesses (i.e. those with receipts not exceeding £150,000) as an alternative to requiring profits and losses to be computed in accordance with generally accepted accounting practice (GAAP). The cash basis rules for property businesses will be similar, but not identical to, those used for smaller trades and professions (see 76 TRADING INCOME — CASH BASIS FOR SMALLER BUSINESSES). One fundamental difference is that the cash basis will be the default method for eligible property businesses, and those wishing to use GAAP will have to opt out of the cash basis. The interest restriction at 76.10 TRADING INCOME — CASH BASIS FOR SMALLER BUSINESSES will not apply to property businesses.

Individuals with more than one eligible property business will be able to choose separately whether to use cash basis or GAAP for each property business. Those with both an eligible UK property business and an eligible overseas property business will be able to make a separate decision on each, as will those with an eligible trade in addition to an eligible property business. Individuals other than spouses or civil partners who jointly own a rental property will be able to decide individually in relation to their respective shares.

See www.gov.uk/government/publications/calculation-of-profits-of-property-b usinesses.'

60

Remittance Basis

Application of the remittance basis

[60.2] At the end of list item (2), a new paragraph is added as follows:

'The prospective new deemed domicile rules at 62.35 RESIDENCE AND DOMICILE, effective for 2017/18 onwards, are not expected to apply for the purpose of applying the "less than £2,000" threshold . If an individual is deemed domiciled in the UK under the new rules, he will nevertheless meet the residence/domicile conditions at (i)–(iii) above for this purpose only, so can still take advantage of the threshold.'

Additional tax charge

[60.10] The first paragraph after the bulleted list is updated to read as follows:

'For 2015/16 onwards, the 7- and 12-year tests continue, but if the individual meets the 17-year test the charge is increased to £90,000. The 17-year test must be applied first, followed by the 12-year test. The 17-year test is to be abolished for 2017/18 onwards as the new deemed domicile rules at 62.35 RESIDENCE AND DOMICILE will render it impossible for someone meeting this test to claim the remittance basis.'

Mixed funds

[60.18] At the end, under a new sub-heading 'Future development', new text is added as follows:

'In conjunction with the prospective new deemed domicile rules at **62.35** RESIDENCE AND DOMICILE, legislation to be included in *FA 2017* will enable an individual who has been taxed on the remittance basis to transfer amounts between overseas mixed fund bank accounts during a limited period without being subject to the offshore transfer rules. This is to allow the different elements within the accounts to be separated, thereby allowing clean capital to be remitted to the UK in priority to income and gains.

This will apply to any individual who was not born in the UK with a UK domicile of origin and who used the remittance basis for any tax year before 2017/18. It is not a condition that the individual has deemed UK domicile under the new domicile rules. It works by disregarding the rule above that if an offshore transfer is made from a mixed fund, it is to be regarded as containing the same proportion of each kind of income or capital as was contained in the fund before the transfer. That rule is disregarded in respect of a transfer of money made from one account (account A) to another (account B) in 2017/18 or 2018/19 which is nominated for this purpose by the individual. It is a condition that, at the time of the nomination, no other transfer from account A to account B has been similarly nominated.

(Autumn tax update, 5 December 2016 at www.gov.uk/government/publicati ons/income-tax-inheritance-tax-and-capital-gains-tax-deemed-domicile-rule.)'

Property used to make qualifying investments

[60.22] At the end, under a new sub-heading 'Future developments', new text is added as follows:

'Legislation to be included in *FA 2017* will make amendments to business investment relief as listed below. These will have effect in relation to investments made on or after 6 April 2017.

- The definition of a qualifying investment (see **60.23** below) will be extended to the acquisition of existing shares (i.e. not just newly issued shares) in a target company.
- Where the target company is *preparing* to trade or hold trading investments the period during which it must actually do so will be extended from two to five years.
- The definition of a qualifying investment will be extended to include a hybrid company, i.e. one that both trades and holds investments in trading companies (or, in either case, is preparing to do so within the next five years).
- It will be clarified that for business investment relief purposes a corporate member of a partnership is not to be regarded as carrying on the trade of the partnership. (It is HMRC's view that this is already the case.)

- Where the two-year start-up rule in **60.24** below is breached due to the target company's ceasing to be operational, the period of grace will be extended so that it does not end until two years after the investor becomes (or ought reasonably to have become) aware of this occurrence.
- The extraction of value rule in **60.24** below will be amended so as to omit the reference to an 'involved company' and thus to apply where value is received from anyone in circumstances directly or indirectly attributable to the investment.

(Autumn tax update, 5 December 2016 at www.gov.uk/government/publicati ons/non-domicile-taxation-business-investment-relief.)'

62

Residence and Domicile

Domicile

[62.35] Under the sub-heading 'Future development', the text is updated to read as follows:

'Legislation is to be included in *FA 2017*, with effect on and after 6 April 2017, to prevent individuals not domiciled in the UK ("non-doms") from being able to claim their non-dom status for tax purposes for an indefinite period of time. There will be two circumstances, as set out below, where an individual will be deemed to be domiciled in the UK for tax purposes.

Firstly, individuals who have been UK resident for at least 15 of the past 20 tax years but are foreign domiciled under general law will be deemed domiciled for all tax purposes in the UK (the '*15-year rule*'). This means that from their 16th tax year of UK residence such individuals will no longer be able to access the remittance basis and will be subject to tax on an arising basis on their worldwide personal income and gains. It follows that an individual who is deemed domiciled under the 15-year rule and who wishes to reset the clock will need to become non-UK resident for at least six complete tax years before becoming UK resident once more. The new rules will be effective from 6 April 2017 irrespective of when the individual arrived in the UK, but do not take effect for as long as an individual remains non-UK resident after 5 April 2017. The deemed domicile of a long-term resident individual for tax purposes has no effect on the domicile status of his children.

Secondly, an individual with a UK domicile at date of birth (i.e. a UK domicile of origin) who has subsequently moved abroad and acquired a domicile of choice overseas will not be able to retain that domicile of choice for tax purposes upon returning to the UK (the '*returning UK dom rule*'). Irrespective of his actual intention, such an individual will be deemed UK domiciled for tax purposes once he becomes UK resident. The rule will affect all returning UK doms on and after 6 April 2017, including those who returned to the UK before that date.

(Autumn tax update, 5 December 2016 at www.gov.uk/government/publicati
ons/income-tax-inheritance-tax-and-capital-gains-tax-deemed-domicile-rule).'

63

Returns

Making tax digital

[63.2] The title of this section, previously 'Digital tax accounts', is updated as
above. The text is updated to read as follows:

'The Government announced at Budget 2015 that it intends to abolish the
personal tax return through the phased introduction of digital tax accounts
over a period leading up to 2020. HMRC will automatically include information it holds about an individual taxpayer's income and circumstances in the
individual's online Personal Tax Account. See the overview at www.gov.uk/g
overnment/publications/making-tax-digital. See also Simple assessment at **6.5**
ASSESSMENTS.

As a significant step toward the above goal, businesses (including property
businesses) will be required from **April 2018** to keep records of income and
expenditure digitally, and to make quarterly reports of income and expenditure, divided into specified categories, to HMRC via compatible software.
Businesses will then be required provide an end-of-year adjustment to HMRC,
again using digital tools, normally within ten months after the end of the
fourth quarter. Those who genuinely cannot go online due to individual
circumstances such as disability, physical location or other reasons will be
exempted from this obligation, as will businesses with an annual turnover of
less than £10,000. See www.gov.uk/government/publications/digital-reporting
-and-record-keeping-for-business-income-tax and www.gov.uk/government/p
ublications/bringing-business-tax-into-the-digital-age-legislation-overview.

Businesses will be able to continue to use spreadsheets for record-keeping, but
will need to combine the spreadsheet with software. Free software will be
available to businesses with the most straightforward affairs. The requirement
to keep digital records does not mean that businesses have to make and store
invoices and receipts digitally. Businesses eligible to use "three line accounts"
(see **59.10** PROPERTY INCOME and **75.18** TRADING INCOME) will be able to submit
their quarterly updates with only three lines of data (income, expenses and
profit). For partnerships with a turnover above £10 million, quarterly reporting is deferred until 2020. Charities will not need to keep digital records,
though this exemption will not extend to their trading subsidiaries. See
www.gov.uk/government/consultations/making-tax-digital-bringing-business-
tax-into-the-digital-age.

Stop press

It was announced at Spring Budget 2017 that the start date for quarterly reporting will be deferred by one year until April 2019 for businesses with an annual turnover not exceeding the VAT registration threshold (currently £85,000). See www.gov.uk/government/publications/making-tax-digital-for-b usiness.'

Notice of enquiry

[63.7] A case citation is updated to read as follows: *R (oao De Silva) v HMRC* CA, [2016] STC 1333.

Completion of enquiry

[63.9] In the first paragraph, a new sentence is added as follows:

'An amendment made by a closure notice is in the nature of an assessment by HMRC (*R (oao Archer) v HMRC* QB, [2017] All ER (D) 166 (Feb)).'

At the end, under a new sub-heading 'Partial closure notices', a new paragraph is added as follows:

'Under legislation to be included in *FA 2017*, with effect in relation both to enquiries open at Royal Assent and to future enquiries, HMRC and taxpayers will be able to conclude discrete matters in an enquiry into a self-assessment return. This will be achieved by the issue by HMRC of a new partial closure notice (PCN) ahead of the final closure of an enquiry. HMRC will be able to issue a PCN either in agreement with the taxpayer, at their own discretion, or when directed to do so by the First-tier Tribunal on application by a taxpayer. HMRC will use the new power in cases where there is tax avoidance, high complexity, or where a large amount of tax is at risk. Where HMRC issue a partial closure notice and amend a return, the taxpayer will have a right to appeal and request postponement of payment of the tax. Tax repayments arising from a PCN will not automatically be repaid, e.g. where tax is due in respect of other issues not covered by the PCN (Autumn tax update, 5 December 2016 at www.gov.uk/government/publications/tax-enquiries-clos ure-rules).'

Partnerships

[63.13] In the final paragraph, the case citation is updated to read as follows: *King v HMRC* FTT (TC 5163), [2016] UKFTT 409 (TC), [2016] SFTD 1033.

65

Seed Enterprise Investment Scheme
The 'no pre-arranged exits' requirement

[65.24] At the end, under a new sub-heading 'Future development', a new paragraph is added as follows:

'Legislation to be included in *FA 2017*, with effect in relation to shares issued on or after 5 December 2016, will exclude from (a) above any arrangements with a view to any shares in the issuing company being exchanged for, or converted into, shares in that company of a different class (Autumn tax update, 5 December 2016 at www.gov.uk/government/publications/income-ta x-streamlining-the-tax-advantaged-venture-capital-schemes).'

70

Share-Related Employment Income and Exemptions

Introduction

[70.1] Under the sub-heading 'Employee shareholder shares', the text is updated to read as follows:

'A new employment status, known as "employee shareholder" status, was introduced in *Growth and Infrastructure Act 2013, s 31* with effect on and after 1 September 2013. Employee shareholders will be issued or allotted at least £2,000 worth of shares in consideration of an employee shareholder agreement. For income tax (and national insurance) purposes, subject to conditions, employee shareholders are deemed to have paid £2,000 for their employee shareholder shares. Subject to conditions, a monetary limit and a lifetime limit, employee shareholder shares are also exempt from capital gains tax when disposed of. These income tax and capital gains tax reliefs are to be abolished by *FA 2017* with effect, in most cases, where the employee shareholder agreement is entered into on or after 1 December 2016. See **70.83** below.'

Restricted shares

[70.4] Under the sub-heading 'Definition of restricted shares', a case citation is updated to read as follows: *Cyclops Electronics Ltd and Graceland Fixing Ltd v HMRC* FTT (TC 5237), [2016] UKFTT 487 (TC), [2016] SFTD 842.

Enterprise Management Incentives

[70.44] In the penultimate paragraph, the telephone number of the Small Company Enterprise Centre is updated to: 0300 123 1083.

Qualifying companies

[70.47] At the end, under the sub-heading 'Informal clearance', the telephone number of the Small Company Enterprise Centre is updated to: 0300 123 1083.

Employee shareholder shares

[70.83] After the first paragraph, a new paragraph is added as follows:

'These income tax and capital gains tax reliefs are to be abolished by *FA 2017* with effect where the employee shareholder agreement is entered into on or after 1 December 2016 (2 December 2016 where independent advice on entering into the agreement was received before 1.30 pm on 23 November 2016) (Autumn Statement, 23 November 2016 at www.gov.uk/government/p ublications/income-tax-and-capital-gains-tax-employee-shareholder-status).'

At the end, a new paragraph is added as follows:

'*ITTOIA 2005, s 385A* above is to be abolished as part of the above-mentioned abolition of income tax and capital gains tax reliefs relating to employee shareholder shares.'

71

Social Investment Relief

Introduction

[71.1] At the end, under a new sub-heading 'Future developments', new text is added as follows:

'Legislation to be included in *FA 2017*, with effect for investments made on or after 6 April 2017, will amend social investment relief as follows.

- The amount of investment a social enterprise can receive over its lifetime under the social investment relief scheme will be fixed at £1.5 million, provided its first 'risk finance investment' is received within seven years after its first commercial sale. Where that condition is not met, the investment limit in **71.33** below, judged over a rolling three-year period, will continue to apply. A '*risk finance investment*' is an investment under the social investment relief scheme, the Enterprise Investment Scheme, the Seed Enterprise Investment Scheme or the Venture Capital Trust scheme.
- Individuals will be eligible to claim social investment relief only if they are independent of the social enterprise.
- Money raised by the social investment relief scheme is not to be used to repay existing loans.
- A 'no disqualifying arrangements' requirement will be introduced, similar to that at **28.40** ENTERPRISE INVESTMENT SCHEME.
- The limit on the number of full-time employees (**71.38** below) will be halved.
- The list of excluded activities at **71.44** below will be extended to include: all energy generation activities; leasing (including letting ships on charter or other assets on hire); the provision of banking, insurance, money-lending, debt-factoring, hire-purchase financing or other finan-

cial services to social enterprises; and the operating or managing of nursing homes or residential care homes. The Government does intend to introduce an accreditation system at a later date to allow investment under the scheme in affordable nursing and residential care homes.

See www.gov.uk/government/publications/income-tax-enlarging-social-investment-tax-relief.'

The 'maximum amount raised' requirement

[71.33] At the end, the text under the sub-heading 'Future development' is superseded by the new text in **71.1** above and is deleted.

Qualifying trade

[71.44] At the end, the text under the sub-heading 'Future developments' is superseded by the new text in **71.1** above and is deleted.

75

Trading Income

Introduction

[75.1] At the end, under the sub-heading 'Future development', the text is updated to read as follows:

'Legislation to be included in *FA 2017* will introduce a £1,000 allowance for trading income for 2017/18 onwards. The new allowance will mean that individuals with trading income of £1,000 or less will no longer need to declare or pay tax on that income. See **75.2A** below.'

Relief for small amounts of income

[75.2A] New text is added as follows:

'Legislation to be included in *FA 2017* will introduce two separate £1,000 allowances for trading income and PROPERTY INCOME (59). The allowance for trading income will also cover any miscellaneous income (within the residual charge to tax at **48.7** MISCELLANEOUS INCOME). The allowances will first have effect by reference to income for 2017/18, which for trading income means the basis period for that year. They will apply to professions and vocations as well as trades, but not to trades, professions, vocations or property businesses carried on in partnership. The allowances will not apply where rent-a-room relief is available (see **59.14** PROPERTY INCOME).

Each of the two allowances operates as follows. Where the individual's gross receipts (i.e. before deducting expenses) do not exceed the £1,000 limit, there is no charge to tax. The individual can, however, elect that this should not apply. Where gross receipts exceed the limit, the individual can elect to use an alternative method of calculating the taxable income. Under this method the charge to tax is on gross receipts less £1,000. Once full relief has been given, or the alternative method applied, there is no tax relief for the expenses that would otherwise have been deductible from receipts in computing taxable income. Under the alternative method, it is for the individual to decide how a £1,000 deduction should be split between two or more trades or property businesses or between trading and miscellaneous income.

Elections must be made by the first anniversary of 31 January following the tax year and have effect only for the tax year for which they are made. There will be an anti-avoidance rule to prevent employers reclassifying payments to employees (or to persons connected with employees) so as to bring those payments within these allowances.

(Autumn tax update, 5 December 2016 at www.gov.uk/government/publicati ons/income-tax-new-tax-allowance-for-property-and-trading-income.)'

Change of accounting date

[75.8] List item (1) is updated to read as follows:

'The period of account ending with the new date does not exceed 18 months. (This condition must be met by the accounts in existence when the tax return is submitted and not by accounts drawn up retrospectively (*Grint v HMRC* FTT (TC 5286), [2016] UKFTT 537 (TC), [2017] SFTD 144).)'

Avoidance schemes

[75.25] The penultimate sentence is updated to read as follows:

'See also *Samarkand Film Partnership No 3 v HMRC* CA, [2017] EWCA Civ 77, *Black Nominees Ltd v Nicol* Ch D 1975, 50 TC 229, *Newstead v Frost* HL 1980, 53 TC 525 and *Flanagan v HMRC* FTT (TC 3314), 82 TC 392, [2014] SFTD 881.'

Trading income provided through third parties

[75.36A] New text is added as follows:

'FA 2017 will include legislation aimed at preventing the use of disguised remuneration schemes by the self-employed. Subject to what is said below about pre-existing loans, the legislation will have effect in relation to 'relevant benefits' arising on or after 6 April 2017. *"Relevant benefit"* means a payment (including a payment by way of a loan), a transfer of money's worth or any other benefit. The legislation will apply both to sole traders and individuals in partnership, and will apply to professions/vocations as it does to trades.

The legislation will have effect where a person (T) carries on a trade and:

(a) T is a party to an arrangement in connection with the trade, or an arrangement otherwise relates to T;

(b)   the arrangement is a means of providing, or is otherwise concerned with the provision of, relevant benefits;

(c)   a relevant benefit thereby arises to T or a person who is or has been connected with T; and

(d)   the relevant benefit represents, or has arisen or derives from, or is otherwise connected with, the whole or part of a payment made (whether or not by T) to another person (or to T acting as a trustee) and in relation to which either Condition A or B below is met.

Condition A is that a deduction for the payment in (d) is made in calculating the profits of the trade or, where the trade is a partnership trade, T's share of the profits. Condition B is that it is reasonable to suppose that the payment is by way of consideration for goods or services provided in the course of the trade, or there is some other connection between the payment and any such provision of goods or services.

The amount of a relevant benefit arising to T will be treated for income tax purposes as profits of the trade for the tax year in which the benefit arises. If T has ceased to carry on the trade in an earlier tax year it will be treated as profits for that earlier year. This will not apply where the relevant benefit is a loan made on ordinary commercial terms and there is no tax avoidance aspect.

If, in pursuance of the arrangement mentioned in (a) above, a relevant benefit arises at any time to a person other than T it is nevertheless treated as arising to T at that time if any of a number of 'enjoyment conditions' is met such that T benefits (or will subsequently benefit) from it. The references here to T include any person connected with him.

Any arrangements a main purpose of which is to secure that the above provisions do not apply are to be disregarded.

Pre-6 April 2017 loans outstanding at 5 April 2019

A loan (or equivalent arrangement) is to be treated as a relevant benefit for the above purposes if it was made before 6 April 2017 (but on or after 6 April 1999) and it remains outstanding immediately before the end of 5 April 2019. The amount of the benefit is the outstanding amount of the loan immediately before the end of 5 April 2019 or, if the relevant benefit is an 'approved fixed term loan' on 5 April 2019, immediately before the end of the approved repayment date. In this case the amount of the relevant benefit is treated as profits of the trade for 2018/19 or, where applicable, the tax year in which the approved repayment date falls. If T has ceased to carry on the trade it is treated as a post-cessation receipt.

A loan is an "*approved fixed term loan*" on 5 April 2019 if it is at that time a qualifying loan (broadly a pre-9 December 2010 loan whose term cannot exceed ten years) which has been approved by HMRC. A person may apply to HMRC in 2018 (or later if HMRC allow in any particular case) for approval of a qualifying loan. HMRC will approve the loan only if they are satisfied that regular repayments have been made (at intervals not exceeding 53 weeks) and that the loan is on commercial terms. There is provision to mitigate any double charge to tax, including where payment has been made under an accelerated payment notice or partner payment notice (see **4.52** ANTI-AVOIDANCE) relating to the relevant benefit.

(Autumn tax update, 5 December 2016 at www.gov.uk/government/publicati ons/disguised-remuneration-self-employed-schemes.)'

Capital expenditure and receipts

[75.38] A case citation is updated to read as follows: *Acornwood LLP v HMRC* UT, [2016] STC 2317.

Compensation, damages etc — receipts

[75.51] In list item (c) (compensation etc relating to capital assets), a new sentence is added as follows:

'A settlement to cover the dilapidated state of let property where the tenant was responsible for upkeep was held to be compensation for the fall in capital value of the property, and not for a loss of rental income, and was thus a capital receipt (*Thornton v HMRC* FTT (TC 5494), [2016] UKFTT 767 (TC)).'

Employee benefit contributions

[75.60] At the end, under a new sub-heading 'Future development', a new paragraph is added as follows:

'In relation to employee benefit contributions (EBCs) made, or to be made, on or after 6 April 2017, legislation to be included in *FA 2017* will deny employers a deduction for EBCs in a period of account unless any associated PAYE and NICs are paid within 12 months after the end of that period. Associated PAYE and NICs are those arising (if any) in respect of benefits provided out of, or by way of, the EBC. It will also be specified that where a deduction would otherwise be allowable for an amount of employees' remuneration paid on or after 6 April 2017 in respect of which EBCs are made (or are to be made), the deduction is to be treated as a deduction in respect of EBCs and not as a deduction in respect of remuneration, thus bringing it within the restrictions. There will also be a new time limit (again in relation to EBCs made, or to be made, on or after 6 April 2017) preventing any deduction of EBCs for a period of account beginning more than five years after the end of the period of account in which the contributions were made (Autumn tax update, 5 December 2016 at www.gov.uk/government/publications/corporati on-tax-and-income-tax-tackling-disguised-remuneration-restricting-tax-relief-for-contributions-to-avoidance-schemes).'

76

Trading Income — Cash Basis for Small Businesses

Introduction

[76.1] The first paragraph is updated to read as follows:

The cash basis has effect for 2013/14 onwards. It is optional, and is available to unincorporated trades, professions and vocations (including those carried on in partnership) with an annual turnover not exceeding the turnover limit. For 2017/18 onwards, the turnover limit is £150,000; previously it was equal to the VAT registration threshold. For recipients of Universal credit, the turnover limit is doubled. See **76.2** below. Certain types of business are excluded from using the cash basis (see **76.3**). Businesses must leave the cash basis the year after their receipts exceed twice the VAT registration threshold (see **76.4** below). In practice, elections to adopt the cash basis will be made via the tax return by ticking a box. If more than one business is carried on by the same person, the combined receipts must be taken into account when applying the turnover test.

Eligibility for cash basis

[76.2] Under the sub-heading 'The turnover limit', the text is updated to read as follows:

'For 2017/18 onwards, the *"turnover limit"* is £150,000. For earlier years it was an amount equal to the VAT registration threshold for the tax year (£83,000 for 2016/17, £82,000 for 2015/16, £81,000 for 2014/15, £79,000 for 2013/14). If, however, the person is a "universal credit claimant" in the tax year, the *"turnover limit"* is doubled, e.g. it is £300,000 for 2017/18 onwards. A *"universal credit claimant"* is an individual who is entitled to the State benefit known as Universal credit for an assessment period (within the meaning of *Welfare Reform Act 2012, Pt 1* or NI equivalent) that falls within the basis period for the tax year in question.

If the basis period for the tax year is less than twelve months, the turnover limit is proportionately reduced. So if, for example, the basis period for 2017/18 or a subsequent year is three months, the turnover limit is £37,500 or, if the person is a universal credit claimant, £75,000.

[*ITTOIA 2005, s 31B(1)(2)(5)–(9); FA 2013, Sch 4 paras 5, 56; SI 2017 No 293*].'

Effects of a cash basis election

[76.4] The text above the sub-heading 'Capital allowances' is updated to read as follows:

'A cash basis election has effect for the tax year for which it is made and, subject to the exceptions below, for every subsequent tax year (regardless of the turnover limit in **76.2** above). A cash basis election that has effect for a tax year has effect in relation to every trade, profession or vocation carried on during the tax year by the person who made the election.

A cash basis election made by a person ceases to have effect for a subsequent tax year (Year S) if:

(a)   the aggregate of the cash basis receipts of each trade, profession or vocation carried on by the person during the tax year (Year R) immediately preceding Year S is greater than £300,000 for Year R *and* the aggregate cash basis receipts exceed the turnover limit for Year S (see further below);

(b)   the person is an excluded person (as in **76.3** above) in relation to Year S;

(c)   the control rule in **76.2** above (i.e. that if the person is an individual who controls a partnership or a partnership that is controlled by an individual, the cash basis election must be made by both) ceases to be satisfied for Year S; or

(d)   there is a change of circumstances relating to any trade, profession or vocation carried on by the person which makes it more appropriate for its profits for Year S to be calculated on an earnings basis and in accordance with generally accepted accounting practice (as in **75.19** TRADING INCOME) and the person duly elects to calculate those profits in that way.

The effect of (a) above is that any person whose cash basis receipts exceed £300,000 for Year R must continue to use the cash basis for Year R (unless (b), (c) or (d) apply to Year R) but must cease to use the cash basis for Year S, *unless* cash basis receipts fall in Year S so that the turnover limit is met for that year.

If the basis period for the tax year in question is less than twelve months, the above figure of £300,000 is proportionately reduced for these purposes.

Where Year S was 2016/17 or an earlier year, an amount equal to twice the VAT registration threshold had effect instead of the figure of £300,000 above. The VAT registration threshold was proportionately reduced for these purposes if the basis period for the year in question was less than twelve months.

As regards (d) above, examples given by HMRC of changes of circumstances include a business that is expanding and wishes to claim more than £500 in interest deductions (contrary to **76.10** below) and a business that wishes to claim loss relief against general income or chargeable gains (contrary to **76.6** below) (HMRC Technical Note, 28 March 2013, Chapter 2 para 10).

In all cases, there is nothing to prevent the person making a further cash basis election for any future tax year for which he is eligible to adopt the cash basis as in **76.2** above.

[*ITTOIA 2005, ss 31B(3)(4)(7)–(9), 31D; FA 2013, Sch 4 paras 5, 56; SI 2017 No 293*].'

Capital expenditure

[76.7] At the end, under a new sub-heading 'Future development', new text is added as follows:

'The following new rule will replace the above for 2017/18 onwards. However, for 2017/18 only, if a deduction would have been allowed under the old rule but not under the new, the old rule will apply so that the deduction *is* allowed. The new rules are that no deduction will be allowed for capital expenditure incurred on, or in connection with:

- the acquisition or disposal of a business or part of a business; or
- the provision, alteration or disposal of any asset that is not a depreciating asset, any asset not acquired or created for use on a continuing basis in the trade, a car, land, a non-qualifying intangible asset or a financial asset.

See www.gov.uk/government/publications/cash-basis-treatment-of-capital.'

78

Transactions in UK Land

Introduction

[78.1] The final two paragraphs are updated to read as follows:

'Some changes were necessary to the UK's double tax treaties. Whilst the majority of these treaties attribute full taxing rights to the UK over profits from land in the UK, some of the older treaties did not. This meant that the *FA 2016* tax charge would not be fully effective, as businesses resident in affected jurisdictions could claim relief from UK tax under the treaty. In this connection, the UK's treaties with Guernsey, Jersey and the Isle of Man were amended with backdated effect from 16 March 2016 (see the list at **26.2** DOUBLE TAX RELIEF).

See also the HMRC Technical Note at www.gov.uk/government/publications/p rofits-from-trading-in-and-developing-uk-land and the guidance at www.gov. uk/government/publications/profits-from-a-trade-of-dealing-in-or-developing-uk-land-guidance.'

80

Unit Trusts etc

Authorised unit trusts (AUTs)

[80.2] At the end, under the sub-heading 'Future development', the text is updated to read as follows:

'Legislation to be included in *FA 2017*, with effect on and after 6 April 2017, will remove the requirement for income tax to be deducted at source from interest distributions from authorised unit trusts, OEICs (see **80.3** below) and investment trust companies (Autumn tax update, 5 December 2016 at www.gov.uk/government/publications/deduction-of-income-tax-from-savings-income).'

Authorised contractual schemes

[80.9A] New text is added as follows:

'An *"authorised contractual scheme"* is a type of collective investment scheme authorised by the Financial Conduct Authority. It may take the form of either a co-ownership scheme or a partnership scheme (as defined). [*Financial Services and Markets Act 2000, s 235A*]. Such schemes are broadly transparent for tax purposes, i.e. the scheme itself incurs no tax liability. This means that its investors are treated as if they had invested directly in the underlying assets of the scheme and are subject to personal taxation accordingly.

Legislation to be included in *FA 2017*, with effect for scheme accounting periods beginning on or after 1 April 2017, will enable operators of co-ownership authorised contractual schemes (CoACS) carrying on a qualifying activity to elect to compute capital allowances and allocate them to investors. *FA 2017* will also introduce rules, with effect on and after Royal Assent, to clarify what is to be treated as an investor's income when a CoACS has invested in an offshore fund (Autumn tax update, 5 December 2016 at www.gov.uk/government/publications/co-ownership-authorised-contractual-s chemes-reducing-tax-complexity).'

81

Venture Capital Trusts

Introduction

[81.1] The second paragraph is updated to read as follows:

'Requirements as to returns, records and providing of information by VCTs are contained in Treasury regulations. [*ITA 2007, ss 272, 284; SI 1995 No 1979; SI 2016 No 1192*].'

Qualifying holdings of a VCT

[81.17] At the end, under the sub-heading 'Informal clearance', the telephone number of the Small Company Enterprise Centre is updated to: 0300 123 1083.

Supplementary provisions

[81.42] After the section headed 'Restructuring', and under a new sub-heading 'Future development', a new paragraph is added as follows:

'Legislation to be included in *FA 2017*, with effect on and after 6 April 2017, will enable a new holding company (as above) that has acquired a company which has previously received VCT funding to use the funding history of the acquired company when considering if follow-on funding is permitted to fund the continuing activities of the acquired company. This is relevant to the permitted maximum age *condition* at **81.12** above and the permitted maximum age *requirement* at **81.34** above (Autumn tax update, 5 December 2016 at www.gov.uk/government/publications/income-tax-streamlining-the-tax-adv antaged-venture-capital-schemes).'

Spring Budget 2017

This is a summary of the most important tax changes in Spring Budget 2017. For more on the Budget, see the Spring Budget 2017 report and the Overview of tax legislation and rates 2017 ('OOTLAR') published by HM Treasury and HMRC (www.gov.uk/Government/publications/spring-budget-2017-overview -of-tax-legislation-and-rates-ootlar).

Personal and Business Tax

The highlights for individuals from the Spring Budget 2017 include:

- the making tax digital threshold for a one-year deferral in digital quarterly reporting will be the VAT threshold,
- the reduction in the dividend nil-rate band from £5,000 to £2,000 in 2018/19,
- the extension of the opportunity to clean-up mixed funds held by non-domiciliaries to cover pre-6 April 2008 foreign income and capital,
- a 25% tax charge on pension transfers to a qualifying recognised overseas pension scheme (QROPS) which take place on or after 9 March 2017.

Personal tax rates and allowances – 2017/18 tax year

Income tax allowances

Personal allowance	£11,500
Income limit for personal allowance	£100,000
Transferable tax allowance (also known as marriage allowance)	£1,150
Married couple's allowance (born before 6 April 1935)	£8,445
Minimum amount of married couple's allowance	£3,260
Income limit for married couple's allowance	£28,000
Blind person's allowance	£2,320

Income tax rates and taxable bands

Rate	
Starting rate for savings: 0%	£1–£5,000
Basic rate: 20%	£1–£33,500
Higher rate: 40%	£33,501–£150,000
Additional rate: 45%	Over £150,000

The savings rates are 0% (starting rate for savings), 0% (savings nil-rate band of £1,000 for basic rate taxpayers and £500 for higher rate taxpayers), 20% (savings basic rate), 40% (savings higher rate), 45% (savings additional rate).

The dividend rates are 0% (dividend nil rate on first £5,000 of dividend income), 7.5% (dividend ordinary rate), 32.5% (dividend upper rate) and 38.1% (dividend additional rate).

In 2017/18 the higher rate will kick in at an income level (before personal allowances) of £45,000 (rather than £43,000 as in 2016/17). This is the biggest above inflation increase to the threshold since it was introduced in 1989.

Scottish taxpayers – income tax bands

The Scottish Government has the power to vary the basic rate, higher rate and additional rate of income tax for non-savings income. It can also create new tax bands. It does not have the power to set the level of the personal allowance, set different rates for different types of income or alter/create/abolish income tax reliefs. These remain reserved by the UK Government.

As was widely expected, the Scottish higher rate threshold (personal allowance plus Scottish basic rate band) in 2017/18 is to be lower than the threshold which applies in the rest of the UK. The Scottish higher rate threshold will be £43,000 in 2017/18 (frozen at the 2016/17 level). The rates of tax and other thresholds remain the same as in the rest of the UK.

This creates a number of mismatches for Scottish taxpayers:

Mismatch	Commentary
Class 1 and Class 4 national insurance contributions	The upper earnings limit for Class 1 and the upper profits limit for Class 4 are aligned with the higher rate threshold which applies in the rest of the UK. Therefore, employed Scottish taxpayers will face a marginal rate of 52% on earnings between £43,000 and £45,000 (Scottish higher rate of 40% plus Class 1 primary rate of 12%). The marginal rate for the self-employed at this profit level will be 49% (Scottish higher rate of 40% plus Class 4 main rate of 9%).
Savings income and dividend income	The income tax rates and thresholds for the savings and dividend income of Scottish taxpayers are the same as for taxpayers in the rest of the UK. This means the starting rate for savings, savings nil-rate band and dividend nil-rate band should be considered for Scottish taxpayers. It also means that Scottish taxpayers may be higher rate taxpayers for non-savings income but basic rate taxpayers for savings income.

Mismatch	Commentary
Rates of capital gains tax	The rate of capital gains tax depends on the remaining basic rate band for income tax. The higher rate threshold for capital gains tax for Scottish taxpayers will remain aligned with the higher rate threshold for the rest of the UK. Therefore it is possible to be a higher rate taxpayer in Scotland but have remaining basic rate band for the purposes of capital gains tax.

National insurance rates and thresholds

Lower earnings limit, primary Class 1	£113
Upper earnings limit, primary Class 1	£866
Primary threshold	£157
Secondary threshold	£157
Upper secondary threshold	£866
Employment allowance (per employer)	£3,000 per year
Employees' primary Class 1 rate between primary threshold and upper earnings limit	12%
Employees' primary Class 1 rate above upper earnings limit	2%
Employers' secondary Class 1 rate above secondary threshold	13.8%
Class 1A rate on employer-provided benefits	13.8%
Class 1B rate on amounts included in a PAYE settlement agreement	13.8%
Class 2 rate	£2.85
Class 2 small profits threshold	£6,025 per year
Class 3 rate	£14.25
Class 4 lower profits limit	£8,164 per year
Class 4 upper profits limit	£45,000 per year
Class 4 rate between lower profits limit and upper profits limit	9%
Class 4 rate above upper profits limit	2%

There is an exemption from secondary Class 1 national insurance contributions (NIC) in relation to employees under 21 and apprentices under 25 years old. The exemption applies until the employee's earnings reach the upper secondary threshold, at which point secondary contributions are due.

Note that the ability to make voluntary Class 3A contributions ceases on 5 April 2017. This was a temporary class of NIC introduced to give people who reached state pension age before 6 April 2016 the opportunity to build up their state pension entitlement by up to £25 per week.

Capital gains tax rates and exempt amount

The annual exempt amount for capital gains tax is increased to £11,300 in 2017/18. The annual exempt amount for trustees in 2017/18 is £5,650.

The capital gains tax rates remain the same for individuals, personal representatives and trustees as they were in 2016/17. The main rates are 10% for basic rate taxpayers and 20% for higher rate taxpayers, trustees and personal representatives. The 'upper rates' of 18% (basic rate taxpayers) and 28% (higher rate taxpayers, trustees and personal representatives) apply to gains on residential property and carried interest. The rate of tax for ATED-related gains remains 28%.

Inheritance tax

The nil-rate band remains £325,000 and the rate of inheritance tax remains unchanged. As announced in Summer Budget 2015, the nil-rate band will remain frozen until 2021/22 at the earliest.

The residence nil-rate band is phased in from 2017/18. The residence nil-rate band applies to reduce the inheritance tax payable on death but is restricted to the value of residential property included in the death estate which is passed to direct descendants.

The amount of the residence nil-rate band available where the date of death falls in 2017/18 is £100,000.

Business owners

Dividend nil rate

Introduced from 2016/17, the dividend nil-rate band (also referred to as the dividend allowance) taxes the first £5,000 of dividend income at 0%, irrespective of the taxpayer's marginal tax rate. At the time it was speculated that this both acted as a simplification measure for the making tax digital agenda and a sweetener for the increase in the effective tax rates for dividend income introduced at the same time.

Given the level of the dividend nil-rate band it is not surprising that the taxpayers who benefitted most from this measure were owner-managers of companies.

As part of the aim to reduce the tax incentive for incorporation, from 2018/19 the dividend nil-rate band will be reduced to £2,000. The Chancellor asserts that at this level most general investors will still pay no tax on their dividends.

It is therefore essential to ensure that individuals maximise their use of the £5,000 dividend nil-rate band in 2017/18.

Appropriations into trading stock

If a trader transfers a business asset into trading stock, the cost of the stock for the purpose of the accounts is the market value at the time it was appropriated. For capital gains purposes, the trader is deemed to have sold the fixed asset at market value. In this instance the trader can elect not to have a capital gains tax disposal but instead to have the cost of the stock reduced by the amount of the chargeable gain. This will reduce the gain to nil but will result in the stock having a lower cost (and therefore a higher trading profit when the stock is eventually sold).

For transfers on or after 8 March 2017, it is no longer possible to make such an election where an allowable loss would arise on an appropriation into trading stock at market value. This means that an allowable loss will be crystallised when the appropriation takes place, and the loss will remain within the capital gains tax rules with respect to how it may be set off in the future. The aim of this provision is to remove the ability of business with loss-making capital assets to obtain an unfair tax advantage by converting those losses into more flexible trading losses.

Where traders have more than one asset they wish to appropriate as trading stock, it will be sensible to consider the timing of this. Where one asset stands at a gain, and one at a loss, it may be advantageous to appropriate the asset standing at a gain before or at the same time as the asset standing at a loss and make no election. This will ensure that the loss arising can be utilised more effectively within the capital gains tax rules.

Partnership tax treatment

Following the August 2016 consultation, Finance Bill 2018 will contain provisions which clarify some aspects of partnership taxation, particularly in relation to profit allocations. The Government is aware that some of the existing rules are unclear or produce an inappropriate outcome and wishes to make both the calculation and reporting of profits simpler. A summary of responses is also expected.

Simplified cash basis for small unincorporated businesses

In line with the summary of responses, with effect from 6 April 2017 the entry and exit thresholds for the simplified cash basis for small unincorporated businesses are being increased. The entry threshold will increase from £83,000 to £150,000. The exit threshold will be £300,000. For Universal Credit claimants both the entry and exit thresholds will be £300,000.

At the same time the rules for deductible capital expenditure under the simplified cash basis will be clarified via the introduction of a statutory list of disallowed expenditure. For 2017/18 profits can be calculated using either the new rules or the existing rules.

Following consultation on the draft legislation, the Finance Bill 2017 clauses will be revised to ensure the rules on the movement from the cash basis to the accruals basis are 'robust'.

Employee issues

Valuation of benefits in kind

As expected from Autumn Statement 2016, the Government will:

- launch a consultation on the valuation of living accommodation,
- publish a call for evidence on the valuation of all other benefits in kind.

Relief for business expenses

A call for evidence will be published in the Finance Bill on the use of income tax relief for employees' business expenses, including those not reimbursed by the employer.

Termination payments

The following changes are to be made to the income tax and NIC treatment of termination payments from 6 April 2018:

- removal of the distinction between the taxation of contractual and non-contractual payments in lieu of notice (PILONs) and make all PILONs both taxable and subject to Class 1 NIC (primary and secondary contributions),
- retention of the £30,000 threshold for termination payments but amounts above that would be subject to secondary Class 1 NIC (no primary Class 1 contributions will be payable by the employee) as well as income tax,
- removal of foreign service relief (except in the case of seafarers).

Although these measures were pre-announced, it is now understood that whilst the bulk of the changes will be legislated in Finance Bill 2017 and NIC Bill 2017 as planned, the abolition of foreign service relief will be deferred to Finance Bill 2018 based on responses to the draft legislation.

Enterprise management incentives

The Government is to seek state aid approval to extend the tax reliefs associated with the enterprise management incentive (EMI) scheme beyond 2018. The last time state aid approval was granted to this scheme was in August 2009.

Property owners

Simplified cash basis for unincorporated businesses

As stated in the January 2017 summary of responses, the simplified cash basis will be extended to unincorporated property businesses from 6 April 2017.

This will be the default method of calculating the property income, unless:

- the landlord makes an election not to use the simplified cash basis (separate elections must be made for different types of property businesses),
- the gross rental income exceeds £150,000,
- the business is carried on by a company, an LLP, a partnership with a corporate partner, a trust or personal representatives,
- business premises renovation allowances have been claimed and there is a balancing adjustment in the tax year.

For those property businesses unwilling or unable to use the simplified cash basis, the accruals basis must be used to calculate the property income.

Where property is owned jointly by spouses or civil partners, if one spouse or civil partner makes an election for the accruals basis to apply then the other spouse/civil partner is excluded from using the simplified cash basis. For all other jointly owned property, each owner can choose whether to elect to use the accruals basis or to remain on the simplified cash basis.

The simplified cash basis for unincorporated property businesses is closely modelled on the simplified cash basis for unincorporated trading businesses, however there are some important differences:

- interest is allowed as a deduction without the application of the £500 limit and the related mixed purpose interest rule (instead interest will be allowed according to the existing rules for landlords, including the restriction of relief for interest in relation to residential properties starting in 2017/18),
- the continued ability to deduct the cost of replacing domestic items in residential properties which applies from 2016/17. The initial cost of capital items used in a dwelling house will not be an allowable expense under the simplified cash basis in the same way as this is not permitted under the accruals basis.

Landlords should consider carefully whether the cash basis is beneficial to them. Whilst simplified accounting may be tempting it could create other issues, particularly in relation to the timing of receipts. For example, if a tenant pays a full year's rent in advance on 31 March then the entire amount must be included in the profits for that year, which could impact areas such as the high income child benefit charge or the abatement of the personal allowance where the adjusted net income exceeds £100,000.

Rent-a-room relief

In a surprise announcement, in summer 2017 the Government will launch a consultation on rent-a-room relief, with a view to better supporting longer-term lodgings.

The reference to longer-term lodging may suggest that the conditions for rent-a-room relief could be altered to ensure it applies to long-term lets only. Currently anyone letting a room in their home on a short-term basis using sharing websites such as Airbnb can receive up to £7,500 per year in rents without paying income tax. When rent-a-room relief was introduced in 1992, this type of short-term letting could not be envisaged and the Government may decide this does not meet the original policy objective.

Non-domiciliaries

At Summer Budget 2015 Chancellor Osborne announced fundamental changes to the tax regime for non-domiciled individuals. They involve deeming an individual to be UK domiciled for tax purposes even though he may be non-domiciled in the UK under general law. The rules will apply for income tax, capital gains tax (CGT) and inheritance tax (IHT).

From 2017/18 it is expected that an individual will be deemed UK domiciled for income tax and CGT:

- if he has been UK resident for at least 15 out of the last 20 tax years, or
- if he was born in the UK with a UK domicile of origin, subsequently left the UK and acquired a non-UK domicile of choice and later becomes resident in the UK

The 20-year 'look-back' period for 2017/18 is 1997/98 to 2016/17. The 'clock' does not restart from 2017/18.

Following the responses to the initial consultation, it was announced that non-domiciliaries:

- caught by the deemed domicile 15-year rule in 2017/18 will be able to rebase their foreign chargeable assets for CGT purposes as at 5 April 2017,
- will have a one-off opportunity to clean-up existing mixed funds within foreign bank accounts (transfers out should be made between 6 April 2017 and 5 April 2019).

Whilst both these measures are good news for the non-domiciliary, they have underlying traps for the unwary that were not obvious at the time of the original announcements.

Clean-up of mixed funds

The change announced affects the cleansing of mixed funds. Based on the latest draft legislation, released on 26 January 2017, it was pointed out by the Chartered Institute of Taxation that mixed funds containing pre-6 April 2008 income and/or capital were excluded from the clean-up. CIOT response (23 Feb 2017), paras 14.6–14.9.

It is confirmed that the Finance Bill 2017 clauses will be amended to include such mixed funds within the opportunity. This probably reflects the original policy intention, since excluding such mixed funds would severely limit its usefulness.

However several uncertainties remain, including: (i) whether it will be possible to clean-up mixed funds based on reasonable estimates of foreign income and capital rather than absolute certainty and (ii) how to determine the composition of any funds remaining in the original bank account following the transfers out. Whilst it is possible that this may be ironed out in the Finance Bill 2017 clauses due for publication on 20 March 2017, it is likely that others will be covered in the subsequent HMRC guidance. Some advisers may, therefore, decide to wait for the publication of the HMRC guidance before beginning to split out mixed funds. The fact that the time limit has been extended to 5 April 2019 (from the originally proposed deadline of 5 April 2018) is helpful here.

Pensions

Money purchase annual allowance

As announced in Autumn Statement 2016, the money purchase annual allowance (MPAA) will be reduced from £10,000 to £4,000. The MPAA is only triggered when a pension scheme member draws income from a flexi-access drawdown fund and it exists to prevent the member reinvesting this money back into a pension, thus obtaining double income tax relief.

Note that the MPAA is **not** triggered if:

*   the member uses the tax-free lump sum only and does not draw income from the taxable portion of the fund,
*   the member's fund is still held under the former 'capped drawdown' arrangement and the withdrawals of income do not exceed the capped amount (if the cap is exceeded, the drawdown fund automatically converts to flexi-access in any case).

Provided members can keep their withdrawals within these conditions, the standard annual allowance of £40,000 applies.

The summary of responses to the November 2016 consultation was expected to be published on 20 March 2017.

Foreign pensions

The announcement at Autumn Statement 2016 that the tax treatment of foreign pensions would be 'more closely aligned' with the UK's domestic pension tax regime was broadly interpreted as being notice that the rule under which only 90% of foreign pension income is subject to UK income tax would be abolished. This was confirmed as correct by the draft legislation published in December 2016.

Specialist schemes for those employed abroad (known as 'section 615' schemes) will be closed to new saving but any lump sums paid out in relation to funds built up before 6 April 2017 will be subject to the current tax treatment.

Foreign pensions – QROPS

A 25% tax charge will be levied on pension transfers to a qualifying recognised overseas pension scheme (QROPS) which take place on or after 9 March 2017.

Although the legitimate use of QROPS is acknowledged, it is noted that the transfer of funds which have benefited from UK income tax relief has provided an opportunity for a tax advantage. QROPS can be located in a lower tax jurisdiction or one which offers less restrictive withdrawal rules. As a result, QROPS schemes have been marketed as tax saving vehicles. The new law aims to preserve the legitimate purpose of transferring pension schemes, whilst penalising the tax avoidance motive.

'Genuine' transfers will be identified if they meet one of the following conditions:

- the QROPS and the person who makes the transfer are resident in the same country, or
- the QROPS and the person who makes the transfer are both resident in a country within the European Economic Area, or
- the transfer is made to a QROPS that is established or sponsored by the employer of the person who makes the transfer.

Transfers which do not meet these conditions will incur a charge of 25% of the value of the transferred.

There will be a five-year window following the transfer during which:

- a transfer which was not chargeable will become so if it ceases to meet the qualifying conditions regarding residence, and
- a charge which was made can be refunded if one of the qualifying conditions starts to apply,
- payments out of the QROPS will be subject to UK tax rules regardless of where the individual then resides.

The administrators of both the UK scheme and the QROPS will be jointly and severally liable to the tax charge. It is expected that it will be deducted from the pension fund on transfer.

Tax planning with QROPS is a niche area, popular with wealthy and internationally mobile individuals. Advisers with clients who may be affected by these changes are advised to study the draft legislation and HMRC guidance at an early stage in view of the immediate changes in the law. Existing QROPS have an early deadline of 13 April 2017 to decide whether they wish to maintain their status.

Investments

ISAs

The ISA limit will be £20,000 in 2017/18 (up from £15,420 in 2016/17), as previously trailed in Budget 2016. The Chancellor used this above inflation increase to partly justify his reduction to the dividend nil-rate band; individuals can purchase shares via an ISA to benefit from the tax-free wrapper.

Venture capital schemes

As announced in Autumn Statement 2016, further minor tweaks to the rules for enterprise investment schemes (EIS), venture capital trusts (VCTs) and seed enterprise investment schemes (SEIS) are expected in Finance Bill 2017:

- clarification to the rules for share conversion rights (for EIS and SEIS shares issued on or after 5 December 2016), which means that the 'no pre-arranged exits' requirement will not apply if a right exists for the conversion or exchange of shares at some future date,
- aligning the VCT rules for follow-on funding to match the rules for EIS,
- a power to enable the rules on share-for-share exchanges for VCTs to be made via secondary legislation.

The summary of responses to the December 2015 consultation on ways of improving the advance assurance service for venture capital schemes is expected to follow the Spring Budget 2017.

Social investments tax relief

As partially announced in Autumn Statement 2016 and further to the draft legislation published on 26 January 2017, the following changes to social investments tax relief (SITR) will apply to investments made on or after 6 April 2017:

- the investment limit for qualifying social enterprises aged up to seven years old will increase to £1.5m,
- the list of excluded activities will be tightened up to include asset leasing and on-lending. Whilst nursing homes and residential care homes will also be classed as excluded activities, the Government intends to revisit these activities in future with the aim of introducing an accreditation system which will allow fundraising via SITR,
- the limit on the number of full-time equivalent employees will be reduced from 500 to 250,
- the use of money raised under the SITR to pay off existing loans will be excluded,
- the law will be clarified so that individuals will be eligible to claim relief under the SITR only if they are independent from the social enterprise,
- a provision will be introduced to exclude investments where arrangements are put in place with the main purpose of delivering a benefit to an individual or party connected to the social enterprise.

Life insurance policies

As expected, legislation will be introduced in Finance Bill 2017 to change the taxation of partial surrenders from life insurance policies in order to prevent excessive tax charges. However, it is interesting that despite consulting on three options, in the end the draft legislation published in December 2016 contained a remedy which was not mentioned in the consultation. Any policy holder who has inadvertently triggered a disproportionate gain will be able to apply to HMRC to have the chargeable event gain recalculated on a just and reasonable basis.

However, the fact that the draft legislation was built around an option which had not been subject to consultation meant that uncertainties remained over the operation of the provision. As such, following comments received, the Finance Bill 2017 clauses will be revised to clarify who can apply, when the application can be made and how the recalculation is to be given effect. These rules will apply from Royal Assent to Finance Act 2017.

Whether this will address the other concerns raised, such as the lack of a statutory right of appeal, remains to be seen.

Savings bonds

As expected, National Savings and Investments (NS&I) will launch a new three-year savings bond in April 2017. It was confirmed in the Spring Budget 2017 that the interest rate will be 2.2% per annum. The bond will be open to those over 16 years of age and the maximum investment will be £3,000. This interest rate is significantly higher than the rates offered by banks and building societies for mainstream savings products and there is likely to be a high take-up amongst basic rate and higher rate taxpayers (who also benefit from the savings nil-rate band).

Administration

Making tax digital

Under making tax digital, businesses will be required to file quarterly income and expense reports digitally. For many businesses this will represent significant extra administration work plus the cost of buying an appropriate software package and extra accountancy fees.

Based on the threshold for the one-year deferral announced in Spring Budget 2017, the main timescales for mandation will be:

- April 2018 – unincorporated businesses (including unincorporated property businesses) with a turnover above the VAT registration threshold (for their income tax obligations only),
- April 2019 – unincorporated businesses (including unincorporated property businesses) with a turnover above £10,000 but below the VAT registration threshold (for their income tax obligations) **plus** all businesses (unincorporated and incorporated) for their VAT obligations,
- April 2020 – all incorporated businesses for their corporation tax obligations.

The use of the VAT threshold as the level for the one-year deferral of quarterly digital reporting is a significant and very welcome development. Anecdotal evidence suggested that HMRC had been reluctant to entertain the idea of using the VAT threshold during the consultation process and it is to its credit that it has listened to advisers on this matter.

For unincorporated businesses it is expected that these requirements will apply to the accounting period beginning on or after 6 April of the relevant year. Therefore, for unincorporated trading businesses it may be possible to extend the deferral period by changing their accounting date. For example a business with turnover below the VAT threshold and an accounting date of 31 March will not have to make quarterly digital reports until the accounting period beginning 1 April 2020. Consideration should of course be given to the change of accounting date rules.

It is not possible to change the accounting date for an unincorporated property business as the income must be reported on a tax year basis.

Making tax digital – tax administration

A further consultation on late submission penalties under the making tax digital regime was due to be published on 20 March 2017.

At the same time, the Government will also consult on the 'design aspects of the tax administration system', with the aim of a consistent approach across the taxes. However it would appear from the draft legislation on administration published in January 2017 that we can expect amendments to be made to the existing statutes rather than using making tax digital as an opportunity for a total rethink of tax administration from a 21st Century perspective.

NIC – collection of arrears

It was announced at Autumn Statement 2016 that from April 2018 NIC would no longer be covered by the Limitation Act 1980. However, this is now expected to be delayed to allow for full consultation. Currently if HMRC wants to recover NIC debt it must raise a protective assessment within six years of the end of the tax year in question. The collection of arrears of tax is not covered by the Limitation Act 1980 so this leads to a mismatch in dealing with historic tax investigations where there is an associated NIC liability.

This is an interesting measure as it will enable HMRC to collect more NIC arrears, but by aligning the treatment for tax and NIC it means it can be badged as a simplification measure and a step towards income tax and NIC alignment.

Note that the position in Scotland is different. There it is already possible to collect NIC debt going back 20 years.

Income tax allowances for property and trading income

The £1,000 'allowances' for property and trading income, previously announced in Budget 2016, come into force in 2017/18. The trading income allowance also covers miscellaneous income from the provision of assets or services.

These work in a similar way to rent-a-room relief in that the first £1,000 of gross trading or property income will be exempt from income tax. If the income exceeds £1,000 the taxpayer will have a choice of:

- deducting the £1,000 'allowance' from their gross income and being taxable on the excess, or
- deducting allowable expenses in the normal way.

To utilise the allowance, the individual must make an election by the first anniversary of 31 January after the end of the tax year (e.g. 31 January 2020 for the 2017/18 tax year).

However, following consultation on the draft legislation published in December 2016, changes will be made in Finance Bill 2017 to prevent the allowances from applying to:

- the income of a participator in a connected close company,
- partnership income.

Employment Taxes

Both generally and from the perspective of employers and their advisers, the spring Budget was refreshingly light on tax measures. Details of those which were included can be found in Chapter 3 of the Spring Budget 2017 document and supported by the OOTLAR which summarises all changes in the pipeline, including those previously announced.

Company cars

There were no changes announced to the company car tax rates that will apply from 2017/18 to 2020/21 as already either enacted or announced in the Autumn Statement.

National Living Wage/National Minimum Wage

The Chancellor in the Budget announced that the National Living Wage will be increased to £7.50 per hour from April 2017. The following table shows all minimum wage rates for all age groups:

Category	Current rate	New rate from 1 April 2017
Workers 25 and over	£7.20 per hour	£7.50 per hour
21–24 year olds	£6.95 per hour	£7.05 per hour
18–20 year olds	£5.55 per hour	£5.60 per hour
16–17 year olds	£4.00 per hour	£4.05 per hour
Apprentices	£3.40 per hour	£3.50 per hour
Accommodation offset	£6.00 per day	£6.40 per day

Personal service companies ('IR35')

As announced in last year's Budget, as from 6 April 2017, where a worker provides his services through a personal service company (PSC) to a public sector body, it will be up to the public sector body (or the agency responsible for paying the PSC) to decide whether or not the special rules for PSCs (known as the IR35 rules) should apply. If the IR35 rules do apply, then the public sector body or agency will deduct the tax due on the resulting deemed employment income payment from the amount due to the PSC under the contract.

In a recent change to proposals for how the public sector body (or agency) should calculate the deemed employment payment, it will be up to them whether they take account of the worker's expenses in calculating that amount. If the expenses are left out of account the worker could still claim a deduction for qualifying expenses in the normal way.

The outline of this measure is covered in HMRC's tax information and impact note.

The list of public bodies who will assume this new responsibility as from 6 April was included as Annex B to the consultation document on this change in approach.

HMRC has also recently published a revised Employment Status Tool to help anyone considering the position of a worker providing services through a PSC to decide whether or not the IR35 rules apply.

Dividend nil-rate band reduction

In a step ostensibly aimed at addressing the unfairness in the differences in tax treatment between employees and those who provide their services through a limited company, the Chancellor announced that the dividend nil-rate band will reduce from £5,000 to £2,000 from 6 April 2018. Although this will indeed impact on the users of personal service companies, it will have a wider impact, affecting anyone receiving dividends of over £2,000 a year, including shareholder directors/employees of many smaller companies.

Pensions

The Budget did not include any new proposals in respect of the lifetime allowance or annual allowance for pension contributions.

However, employers of internationally mobile employees may well want to be aware that there is a new 25% charge on pension scheme members if they make a transfer from a UK-registered pension scheme to a Qualifying Recognised Overseas Pension Scheme (QROPS). It will apply to transfers taking place on or after 9 March 2017. This charge does not apply if **any** of the following apply:

• the member is resident in the same country in which the QROPS receiving the transfer is established,
• the member is resident in a country within the European Economic Area (EEA) and the QROPS is established in a country within the EEA,
• the QROPS is an occupational pension scheme sponsored by the individual's employer,
• the QROPS is an overseas public service pension scheme and the member is an employee of an employer that participates in the scheme,
• the QROPS is set up by an international organisation to provide benefits for or in respect of past service as an employee of the organisation and the member is an employee of that international organisation.

This means that an employee making a transfer from a registered scheme into a QROPS as a consequence of a cross-border change in employment will often be outside the new charge.

Other changes to be included in Finance Bill 2017

The OOTLAR document includes confirmation that a number of previously announced measures of particular interest to employers are still on course to be included in Finance Bill 2017.

Benefits in kind

During the summer last year there was a consultation on proposals to align the date for 'making good' on benefits in kind. If an employee 'makes good' (repays) an amount to the employer in respect of a benefit in kind, the cash equivalent is reduced by the amount made good. The date by which the employee must 'make good' in order to reduce a benefit varies according to the benefit provided.

In para 1.6 of OOTLAR, HMRC confirms that Finance Bill 2017 will include legislation to set the aligned date to be 6 July following the end of the tax year. This change will apply for benefits provided in 2017/18 onwards.

Salary sacrifice

With effect from 6 April 2017, salary sacrifice arrangements, described as 'optional remuneration arrangements', may be used to achieve tax and NIC savings only in the case of:

* employer pension contributions and advice,
* employer-provided childcare,
* cycle-to-work schemes,
* ultra-low emission company cars.

Transitional provisions apply where the salary sacrifice arrangement was in place before 6 April 2017. See para 1.7 of OOTLAR.

Termination payments

The Autumn Statement last year included details of the expected changes to the treatment of termination payments. In para 1.8 of today's OOTLAR, HMRC indicates that although the main changes to the tax and NIC treatment of termination payments will be legislated in the Finance Bill 2017, proposals to abolish foreign service relief will be deferred to the Finance Bill 2018.

Proposal dropped – sanction for hiring illegal workers

In last year's Budget the Chancellor announced an intention to temporarily deny the NIC employment allowance to employers taking on workers who do not have a legal right to work in the UK. Following consultation, this proposal has been dropped. Any employer taking on such workers already faces significant civil penalties of up to £20,000 per illegal worker.

Upcoming consultations

The OOTLAR document gives details of a number of consultations on possible future changes to employment taxes, due to be published on 20 March 2017:

* a call for evidence on employees' expenses,
* consultation on proposal to modernise the tax treatment of employer-provided living accommodation and board and lodgings

a call for evidence on exemptions and valuation methodology for employer-provided benefits in kind.

Corporation Tax

In the spirit of moving towards a single fiscal event in the autumn, the Spring Budget 2017 does not set out major changes to the taxation of companies. Minor amendments have been made to a number of announcements made in previous years, details of which are provided below.

Further information on some of the announcements will be available when the Finance Bill 2017 is published.

Appropriations to trading stock

Currently, if a fixed asset is appropriated into trading stock, then the 'cost' of the stock for the purposes of the accounts is the market value at the time it was introduced. For chargeable gains purposes, there is a deemed disposal of the fixed asset at market value. In this instance an election can be made to reduce the cost of the stock by the amount of the chargeable gain, rather than triggering a disposal. This will reduce the gain to nil but will result in the stock having a lower cost, and therefore a higher trading profit, when the stock is eventually sold.

For transfers made on or after 8 March 2017, it is no longer possible to make such an election where an allowable loss would arise on an appropriation into trading stock at market value. This means that an allowable loss will be crystallised when the appropriation takes place, and the loss will remain within the chargeable gains rules with respect to how it may be set off in the future. The aim of this provision is to remove the ability of businesses with loss making capital assets to obtain an unfair tax advantage by converting those losses into more flexible trading losses.

Where companies have more than one asset that may be appropriated to trading stock, it will be sensible to consider the timing of any appropriation. Where one asset stands at a gain, and one at a loss, it may be advantageous to appropriate the asset standing at a gain before or at the same time as the asset standing at a loss and make no election. This will ensure that the loss arising can be utilised more effectively within the chargeable gains rules.

Review of R&D regime

The UK has a comprehensive regime to encourage companies to invest in research and development.

Following a review, the Government has announced that administrative changes will be made to the research and development expenditure credit (RDEC) to increase certainty and to simplify claims. Action will also be taken to increase awareness of R&D tax credits among SMEs. Further details on the changes, or indeed when they are likely to have effect, have not been provided.

Offshore property developers

Legislation was introduced by Finance Act 2016, ss 76–77 to ensure non-resident developers of UK land are subject to UK corporation tax on the profits generated by this activity. This was intended to create a level playing field between UK and foreign-based developers. The original legislation excluded profits arising from contracts entered into before 5 July 2016. The Government did not anticipate that profits arising many months or years later as a result of these contracts would not be subject to UK corporation tax. Amendments have been made to ensure that all profits recognised in a period of account beginning on or after 8 March 2017 are taxed irrespective of when the contract was entered into. Where the period of account straddles 8 March 2017, then the amounts arising between 8 March 2017 and the end of the straddling period are also taxed.

Plant and machinery leasing

Current rules under GAAP treat leased assets as either finance leases or operating leases. Finance leases are capitalised on the balance sheet as fixed assets, with a matching lease obligation in creditors. Assets subject to operating leases are off balance sheet assets.

IFRS 16, which is the new leasing standard issued by the International Accounting Standards Board, comes into effect on 1 January 2019. This standard will radically alter the GAAP treatment of lessees of most assets, although lessors will still maintain a distinction between finance and operating leases. There are exceptions within the standard for leases of 12 months or less and low value items.

The impact for lessees will be to increase the level of debt and the value of the asset base on the balance sheet, as all leases must be capitalised. The timing of debits recognised in the accounts on operating leases will be accelerated, even though the payments for hire of the asset are likely to be uniform over the lease. Rental expenses on leases which are currently classified as operating leases will be replaced by depreciation and front loaded interest charges. Companies using IFRS may need to model the effect on their gearing, earnings per share and debt covenants as well as many other financial metrics and ratios.

The Government will launch a consultation in Summer 2017, building on the discussion document published in Summer 2016. The Government intends to maintain the current system of lease taxation, rather than changing the tax system to match the accounting. This would seem to be the most sensible approach as it should avoid awkward and complex transitional adjustments. However, one downside of this approach will be to create differences between the P&L debits and the amounts deductible for tax, requiring greater measurement and tracking of temporary differences within deferred tax.

It should be noted that some changes to the rules on long funding leases and certain anti-avoidance rules on leasing will be required as they are linked to current accounting definitions.

Withholding tax amendments

Withholding tax exemption for debt traded on multilateral trading facility

UK tax at the basic rate of 20% must be withheld from certain payments of annual interest. It was announced that an exemption will be introduced for interest on debt traded on a multilateral trading facility. The purpose of the exemption, which is subject to consultation in Spring 2017, is to further the development of UK debt markets.

Double taxation treaty passport scheme

HMRC launched a Double Taxation Treaty Passport (DTTP) scheme for overseas corporate lenders applicable to loans taken out on or after 1 September 2010. The lender must be resident in a country with which the UK has a double taxation treaty that includes an interest or income from a debt claim article. The existence of a 'Treaty Passport' simplifies the process whereby a UK borrower is able to access reduced rates of withholding tax. In order to assist businesses with raising finance, the Government announced today an intention to renew and extend the administrative simplifications of the DTTP scheme. Guidance and the revised terms and conditions applying to the scheme will be published on GOV.UK on 6 April 2017.

Large business risk review

A consultation document is due to be published in Summer 2017 which aims to review HMRC's processes for assessing the risk profile of large businesses. The Government also wants to consider ways of promoting stronger compliance. Unfortunately, further details have not been provided alongside today's announcement.

Patient capital

'Patient capital' is a term used to describe a long-term capital investment in a growing innovative business. The investor is willing to make a financial investment in a business with no expectation of generating a quick profit, however it is possible that more substantial returns will be generated at some point in the future.

The Patient Capital Review was launched by HM Treasury and the Department for Business, Energy & Industrial Strategy (BEIS) in January 2017 as part of the Government's aim to build a modern industrial strategy. The review did not previously include consideration of the tax measures linked with patient capital for growing businesses. The Chancellor announced today that a consultation will be launched in Spring 2017, which will review the tax reliefs aimed at encouraging investment and entrepreneurship. Specific reliefs have not been mentioned, but it is assumed that it could include EIS reliefs, SEIS reliefs, VCT reliefs, entrepreneurs' relief and investors' relief.

The final recommendations from the review will be presented to the Chancellor ahead of Autumn Budget 2017.

Creative sector tax reliefs

It was confirmed today that the Government will seek State Aid approval for the continued provision of high-end television, animation and video games tax reliefs beyond 2018.

Amendments to measures previously announced

A number of measures that have been announced in the past are subject to minor amendments. Details are provided below.

Deductibility of interest

Following announcements at Budget 2016, plus a period of consultation, draft legislation was published on 5 December 2016 and 26 January 2017 to restrict the tax deduction available to companies in respect of interest and similar items.

From 1 April 2017, a group will have its interest expense restricted to a maximum deduction of 30% of earnings before interest, tax, depreciation and amortisation (EBITDA) that is taxable in the UK. The legislation also includes a modified debt cap replacing the existing worldwide debt cap to ensure that the UK net interest deduction cannot exceed the total net interest expense of the worldwide group. An optional group ratio rule based on the net interest to EBITDA ratio of the worldwide group may result in a greater deduction in some circumstances.

Alternative rules apply to infrastructure companies which may have the effect of largely taking them outside the rules with no interest restriction even though they may be highly geared.

Groups with net interest expense of £2m or less will be unaffected by these rules.

The Government has announced a series of detailed amendments to eliminate 'unintended consequences' and reduce 'unnecessary compliance burdens' as follows:

- changes to the modified debt cap to prevent certain restrictions for carried forward interest expenses,
- the alternative rules for public infrastructure groups will be simplified to eliminate the need to compare levels of indebtedness of non-qualifying group companies. Transitional rules will apply in the first year to allow any necessary restructuring to obtain the more favourable alternative treatment,
- the rules on guaranteed debt have been amended including those in relation to intra-group guarantees,
- income and expenses from dealing in financial instruments will be included in the definition of interest for banking trades,
- special rules will allow insurers to compute interest on an amortised cost basis as an alternative to fair value accounting.

These changes will be reflected in Finance Bill 2017 and will have effect from 1 April 2017.

Reform of the substantial shareholdings exemption (SSE)

Following a period of consultation, amendments will be made to the SSE reforms included in the draft Finance Bill 2017, which were originally announced at Autumn Statement 2016. Whilst we do not yet have details, the latest changes are expected to provide further clarity and certainty and take effect from 1 April 2017.

Reform of loss relief

Reforms to the loss relief regime were originally announced at Budget 2016. Legislation was included in the draft Finance Bill 2017, with further draft legislation published on 26 January 2017. The latest changes include provisions for oil and gas companies and oil contractors. All reforms take effect from 1 April 2017.

Patent box

It was announced at Autumn Statement 2016 that the patent box rules would be revised by Finance Bill 2017 where two or more companies work in collaboration on R&D projects under a cost-sharing arrangement. The definition of a cost-sharing arrangement will be narrowed and the way in which payments are structured under the cost-sharing arrangement will be altered. The changes will take effect from 1 April 2017.

Hybrid mismatches

FA 2016 introduced legislation to tackle aggressive tax planning involving the use of hybrid and other mismatch arrangements. It was announced in a technical note at Autumn Statement 2016 that two minor amendments would be made to the hybrid mismatch rules, and a TIIN has been published providing further details. The first change helps to relieve the administrative compliance burden in respect of financial instruments and the second change ensures that amortisation deductions are not treated as giving rise to a mismatch. The changes take effect from 1 January 2017.

Grassroots sports

It was originally announced at Autumn Statement 2015 that companies will be able to claim a deduction for contributions to grassroots sports in certain circumstances. It was announced today that the treatment of a sport governing body will be extended by Finance Bill 2017 to include its 100% subsidiaries. These provisions will have effect from 1 April 2017.

Tax relief for museums and galleries

As announced at Budget 2016, Finance Bill 2017 will introduce a new tax relief for museums and galleries. Further details on the operation of the relief were announced at Autumn Statement 2016. Following consultation on the legislation contained in draft Finance Bill 2017, it was announced today that the relief will be extended to allow for exhibitions which have a live performance as part of the exhibition, provided the live performance is not the main focus.

Corporation tax in Northern Ireland

For a number of years, the Government has been working with the Northern Ireland Executive to pursue the introduction of an Northern Ireland corporation tax rate of 12.5% from April 2018. It was confirmed today that all small and medium-sized enterprises trading in Northern Ireland will be given the potential to benefit. Anti-abuse provisions together with other minor drafting improvements will feature in the revised legislation contained in Finance Bill 2017.

Inheritance Tax, Trusts and Estates

The Spring Budget was light on new tax proposals overall, and inheritance tax did not feature at all. However, it is worth being reminded of some new measures due to be introduced with effect from April 2017 which have been previously announced and the budget included some new points relating to pensions and trusts which will be of interest to private client practitioners.

Trusts default rate of income tax

The OOTLAR, para 1.1 makes a somewhat cryptic reference to a 'default rate' of income tax which will apply to trustees. This is not a new rate of tax for trusts but requires some explanation.

With effect from 6 April 2017, the Scottish parliament will be able to set a Scottish rate of income tax to apply to non-savings, and non-dividend income in Scotland. This 'main rate' of tax will apply to individuals' employment, trade, pensions and property income. It does not apply to trusts.

To correspond with the creation of a main rate for Scottish taxpayers, the same term will apply to the non-savings, non-dividend income of individuals in the rest of the UK. The inference is, of course, that the main rates for each part of the UK could diverge in due course.

The regional authority over tax rates does not extend to the standard rates applied to trusts or non-residents. Hence the introduction of a new term, 'default rate' which describes the standard rate applied to non-savings, non-dividend income of those entities. For trusts, this category is primarily property income.

Although no additional measures are proposed at present, the separation of the rates does pave the way for different rates for trusts in the future.

Inheritance tax and the non-domicile rules

Practitioners are reminded that the Finance Bill 2017 will legislate for the reform of the domicile rules which was initially outlined in the Summer Budget 2015. The new rules will take effect from 6 April 2017. Draft legislation was published in January 2017 and the OOTLAR, para 1.26 confirmed that the measures will go ahead with only minor amendment. For inheritance tax purposes, the key changes are:

- a non-UK domiciled person (non-dom) will become deemed domiciled after being UK resident for 15 of the past 20 years (instead of 17 years out of 20 currently),
- a person with a UK domicile of origin who has acquired a different domicile of choice will be deemed domiciled while they are UK resident,

- inheritance tax will be charged on all UK residential property even when held by a non-dom through an offshore structure.

The standard non-dom tax planning strategy of placing foreign property in a non-UK resident trust before the individual becomes deemed domiciled continues to be an effective way of minimising UK tax, and is, in fact specifically confirmed in the OOTLAR and draft legislation. However, this strategy will no longer work for a non-dom who had a UK domicile of origin but becomes deemed domiciled when UK resident.

Inheritance tax and residence nil-rate band

For deaths after 6 April 2017 an increase in the nil-rate band will be available where the value of a residence is bequeathed to direct descendants.

VAT, other Indirect Taxes and Duties

VAT

Registration and deregistration thresholds

With effect from the 1 April 2017 the following thresholds will apply:

- VAT registration threshold will increase from £83,000 to £85,000.
- The VAT registration threshold for relevant acquisitions from other EU member states will also increase from £83,000 to £85,000.
- The VAT deregistration threshold will increase from £81,000 to £83,000.

Use and enjoyment provisions for business to consumer mobile phone services

The Government stated that it intends to remove the use and enjoyment provisions that alleviate the need for UK VAT to be charged on business to consumer (B2C) mobile phone services provided to a UK resident person travelling outside of the EU.

The change is intended to resolve the inconsistency where UK VAT is applied to mobile phones used by UK residents when in the EU, but not when the mobile phone is used outside the EU.

The changes are intended to prevent telecommunication providers from using the inconsistency to avoid accounting for UK VAT and it will bring the UK into line with the internationally agreed approach.

Secondary legislation and a TIIN will be published before the summer recess.

Fraud in the provision of labour in the construction sector

The Government announced that it intends to have a consultation on possible options to combat missing trader fraud in the provision of labour in the construction sector. One option would be to extend the scope of the domestic reverse charge mechanism to include labour provided in the construction industry so that the recipient accounts for any VAT due.

A consultation document will be published on 20 March 2017.

Split payment model

Certain overseas businesses avoid paying UK VAT on goods supplied online which undercuts UK retailers and abuses the trust of UK customers purchasing goods via an online marketplace.

The Government had previously announced the introduction of measures that are intended to combat VAT avoidance by online businesses in Autumn Statement 2016. The Government has now announced that it would like to collect evidence on whether it would be appropriate to introduce a new VAT collection mechanism in respect of online sales using technology that enables VAT to be collected and remitted directly to HMRC at the time the sale takes place.

This is commonly referred to as the split payment method, where the supplier will receive the net amount and the VAT will be remitted directly to HMRC. The Government believes that this will be another step that could be used to tackle VAT avoidance by overseas online suppliers selling goods to UK consumers.

A 'call for evidence' will be published on 20 March 2017.

Penalty changes in fraud cases

The Government announced in Autumn Statement 2016 that legislation will be included in Finance Bill 2017 introducing a penalty for participating in VAT fraud. The Government consulted on the draft legislation and as a result they have made some minor amendments to improve clarity of the measure and to limit the naming of a company officer to instances where the amount of tax due exceeds £25,000. The new penalty will come into effect from the date of Royal Assent to the Finance Bill.

Energy and transport taxes

Vehicle Excise Duty (VED)

The VED for cars, motorcycles and vans registered before 1 April 2017 will be increased by the Retail Price Index (RPI) with effect from 1 April 2017.

HGV VED and Road User Levy

These rates will be frozen with effect from 1 April 2017. The Government has requested evidence be provided in respect of updating the existing HGV Road User Levy and they will formally issue this request in Spring 2017. The Government also stated that it intends to work with the industry in order to update the levy so that it will reward hauliers that plan their routes efficiently and incentivise hauliers to make efficient use of the roads and improve air quality.

Red diesel

The Government announced that it intends to request evidence on the use of red diesel in order to improve its understanding of eligible industries and their use of red diesel. The Government would specifically like to receive evidence from urban red diesel users.

The call for evidence will be published on 20 March 2017.

Air Passenger Duty (APD)

The rate of APD for the year 2018/19 will increase in line with the RPI. The rates for 2019/20 will be provided in Autumn Budget 2017 in order to give airlines sufficient notice of the increase.

Carbon pricing

The Government announced that it remains committed to carbon pricing in order to assist with decarbonising the power sector. UK prices are currently determined by the EU Emissions Trading System and Carbon Price Support.

With effect from 2021/22, the Government intends to target a total carbon price and will set the specific tax rate at a later date in order to give businesses greater clarity on the total price that they will be required to pay. Further details on carbon prices for the 2020s will be set out at Autumn Budget 2017.

Levy control framework

The Government is aware that it will need to limit the cost for businesses and households as the UK decarbonises its energy supplies. The Levy Control Framework has already been assisting with controlling the costs of low carbon subsidies in recent years and it will be replaced by a revised set of controls. Details of these new controls will be provided later in 2017.

Insurance Premium Tax (IPT)

The Government has reconfirmed its announcement in Autumn Statement 2016 that it will be introducing anti-forestalling measures when the standard rate increases to 12% with effect from June 2017.

The current anti-forestalling legislation is no longer relevant so new legislation will be introduced with effect from 8 March 2017.

Under the anti-forestalling measure:

(a) businesses will be required to charge the new rate of IPT on a premium received between the announcement and the rate change if the cover under the insurance contract starts on or after the date of the change. This is done by deeming the premium to be received on the date of the rate change. However, this does not apply where it is the insurer's normal commercial practice to receive pre-payments of premiums, and

(b)   businesses will be required to charge the new rate of IPT on a
       pro-portion of a premium received between the announcement and the
       rate change if the cover under the insurance contract starts before the
       rate change and extends until after the first anniversary of the rate
       change. This is done by deeming a proportion of the premium to be
       received on the rate change date. That proportion is the amount which
       relates to the period of cover which runs from the first anniversary.
       However, this does not apply where it is the insurer's normal commer-
       cial practice to issue contracts for periods longer than one year.

Environmental taxes

Aggregates levy

The current rate of £2 per tonne will remain in effect.

Landfill tax

The value of the Landfill Communities Fund (LCF) for 2017/18 will remain
unchanged at £39.3m and the cap on contributions made by landfill operators
will increase to 5.3%. The current cap will be maintained, subject to
consideration of Landfill Tax receipts, continuing progress in reducing the level
of unspent funds that are held by environmental bodies and the proportion of
the LCF that are spent on administration costs.

The Government announced that it intends to consult on extending the scope
of landfill tax to cover illegal waste disposals that are made without the
required permit or licence.

Landfill tax – definition of taxable disposal

The Government previously announced at Budget 2016 that legislation will be
introduced in Finance Bill 2017, and in secondary legislation, to amend the
definition of a taxable disposal for landfill tax. The Government has consulted
in the draft legislation and changes have been introduced in order to clarify the
tax treatment of material disposed of at landfill sites and give greater certainty
to landfill site operators. The draft legislation has been restructured to simplify
and improve ease of comprehension. The measure will come into effect after
Royal Assent to Finance Act 2017 and the changes will apply to disposals to
landfill in England, Wales and Northern Ireland.

Alcohol and tobacco

Alcohol duty rates and bands

The duty rates on beer, cider, wine and spirits will increase by the RPI with
effect from 13 March 2017.

The Government announced that it intends to have a consultation on:

(a)   introducing a new duty band for still cider that has a just below 7.5% abv in order to target white ciders, and

(b)   the impact of introducing a new duty band for still wine and made-wine between 5.5 and 8.5% abv.

Tobacco duty rates

The Government has previously announced in Budget 2014 that tobacco duty rates will increase by 2% above RPI inflation and this change will come into effect from 6pm on 8 March 2017.

Minimum Excise Tax

The Government announced that it will be introducing a Minimum Excise Tax for cigarettes that is intended to target the cheapest tobacco and promote fiscal sustainability. The rate will be set at £268.63 per 1,000 cigarettes. The new tax will come into effect from 20 May 2017.

Tobacco: Illicit Trade Protocol – licensing of equipment and the supply chain

Following the announcement made in Autumn Statement 2015 and following technical consultation on the draft legislation produced in December 2016, legislation will be introduced in Finance Bill 2017 that will be intended to control the use and ownership of tobacco manufacturing machinery in the UK. The changes are intended to prevent the illicit manufacture of tobacco products in the UK by introducing powers to establish a licensing regime for this type of machinery. Powers will also be introduced to provide for forfeiture of unlicensed tobacco manufacturing machinery and penalties for failure to comply with the conditions of a licence. The legislation will take effect from the date of Royal Assent.

Heated tobacco products

As announced in Budget 2016 the Government will be consulting on the duty treatment of heated tobacco products. The consultation will be launched on 20 March 2017 and the consultation document should be available on this date.

Soft drinks levy

The levy for sugar that is added to drinks with a total sugar content of at least five grams per 100 millilitres will be set at 18 pence per litre and drinks with a sugar content of at least eight grams will be set at 24 pence per litre. Manufacturers and importers who take reasonable steps to reduce the sugar content will pay less or alleviate the need to pay the levy at all.

Following consultation the legislation has been revised to include a criminal offence for evasion of the levy. Minor amendments have also been made to improve clarity. The levy will take effect from April 2018.

Gaming duty

Gross gaming yield (GGY)

The Government previously announced in Budget 2016 that they will include legislation in Finance Bill 2017 that will raise the GGY bandings for Gaming Duty in line with inflation based on the RPI. The revised GGY will be used to calculate the amount of Gaming Duty due for accounting periods starting on or after 1 April 2017.

Remote gaming duty – freeplays

The Government announced in Budget 2016 that it will include legislation in Finance Bill 2017 to amend the definition of gaming payment and prizes and change the tax treatment of freeplays for remote gaming duty. The Government consulted on the changes and the draft legislation has been amended to ensure that the change is proportionate. The legislation is intended to ensure that freeplays used to participate in remote gaming will have a value as stakes when calculating the dutiable profit of the operator and freeplays given as prizes will not be deductible.

Anti-Avoidance

Promoters of Tax Avoidance Schemes (POTAS)

The Government announced that it intends to introduce new legislation that is intended to ensure that promoters of tax avoidance schemes cannot circumvent the new POTAS regime by reorganising their business to either share control of a promoting business or putting persons between the promoting business and themselves.

Strengthening tax avoidance sanctions and deterrents

The Government previously announced in Autumn Statement 2016 that a new penalty will be introduced in respect of a person who has enabled another person or business to use a tax avoidance arrangement that is later defeated by HMRC. The Government also intends to remove the defence of having relied on non-independent advice as taking reasonable care when HMRC considers whether penalties will be levied on a person or business that has used a tax avoidance arrangement.

The changes relating to reasonable care come into effect at Royal Assent and apply to inaccuracies in documents relating to tax periods which begin on or after 6 April 2017. The penalty for enablers will apply prospectively to enabling activity after Royal Assent.

Disclosure of indirect tax avoidance schemes

The Government announced in Autumn Statement 2016 that legislation will be introduced in Finance Bill 2017 that is intended to strengthen the regime for disclosing indirect tax avoidance arrangements. The provisions will make scheme promoters primarily responsible for disclosing schemes to HMRC and the scope of the legislation will be extended to include all indirect taxes including the Soft Drinks Levy. These measures will become effective from 1 September 2017.